Mencken, Henry L.
Mencken's last
campaign

Mencken's Last Campaign

H. L. Mencken on the 1948 Election

Books by Joseph C. Goulden

The Best Years **1976**
The Benchwarmers **1974**
Meany **1972**
The Superlawyers **1972**
The Money Givers **1971**
Truth Is the First Casualty **1969**
Monopoly **1968**
The Curtis Caper **1965**

Mencken's Last Campaign

H.L. Mencken on the 1948 Election

Edited with an Introduction by

Joseph C. Goulden

THE NEW REPUBLIC BOOK COMPANY, INC.

Washington, D.C.

Published in the United States of America in 1976
by The New Republic Book Company, Inc.
1220 Nineteenth St., N.W., Washington, D.C. 20036

This book consists in part of articles by H.L. Mencken that appeared in *The Baltimore Sun* between June and November of 1948. The New Republic Book Company wishes to thank the Mercantile-Safe Deposit and Trust Company (Baltimore, Maryland), Trustee under the Will of Henry L. Mencken, for permission to reprint them.

The New Republic Book Company also wishes to acknowledge the following for permission to reprint "The Wallace Paranoia": From THE VINTAGE MENCKEN, gathered by Alistair Cooke. Copyright © 1955 by Alfred A. Knopf, Inc. Reprinted by permission of the publisher.

Library of Congress Cataloging in Publication Data

Mencken, Henry Louis, 1880-1956.
Mencken's last campaign.

1. Presidents—United States—Election—1948—Collected works. I. Title.
E815.M45 329'.023'730918 76-10128
ISBN 0-915220-18-0

Printed in the United States of America

For Trey and Jimmy Goulden
Two good guys I'm proud to have as sons.

Sources and Acknowledgments

Put most directly, I am a Mencken nut and have been since the winter night in 1956 when mutual friends, Ron and Marian Wolk, took me to 1524 Hollins Street in Baltimore for a visit with HLM's brother August. A retired engineer, with wondrously flamboyant stories about his experiences in Latin America (some of them undoubtedly tinged with truth) Mr. August took a frosted bottle of gin from the freezing compartment of the refrigerator, poured martinis *sans* vermouth, and made us at home. God, I thought, I'm really *here*; that bell jar next to me is the one Sara Haardt gave to Mr. Mencken when they married. And *his* cigars have been in that ash tray. Sadly, I was so enthralled at the fact of my presence in the Mencken home that whatever anecdotes Mr. August might have told have slipped away into the crevices of my memory and are nowhere to be found.

No matter. For almost two decades I have collected—and read, and relished—every bit of Menckeniana that has come into reach. Last year during work on another book, about the postwar period, I came across an obvious but neglected trove of Mencken material—the articles that comprise the core of this book. They are veritably the last hurrah of the man who stood as America's premier political reporter during the first half of the century, and as I read them I decided they deserved a wider audience.

Some people who helped in the process, and to whom I am grateful, are William G. Frederick, vice president of the Mercantile-Safe Deposit & Trust Company, which is trustee under Mr. Mencken's will; William Koshland, of Alfred A. Knopf, Inc., Mr. Mencken's publisher; William Bernard and Mary Lenz of the *Baltimore Sunpapers*, for arranging permission to use material copyrighted by the A.S. Abell Company, the *Sun* parent company; William H. Y. Knight, Jr., George C. Dorsch, and Paul Ward, former associates of Mr.

Mencken's at the *Sunpapers;* Marquis Childs; Wilbur McGill, of the Enoch Pratt Free Library, Baltimore; Carl D. Brandt, agent and friend, and Joan Tapper, an editor of infinite patience and tenacity. The columns are taken from Mr. Mencken's scrapbooks in the Mencken room at the Pratt Library and are the final versions of each day's article. The Alistair Cooke quotations are from his article in the May 1956 *Atlantic Monthly,* "The Last Happy Days of H.L. Mencken."

Arlington, Virginia
February 1976

JOSEPH C. GOULDEN

Contents

"All Bla-a-ah."

At sixty-eight he had the physical grace of a discarded beer barrel. Ovoid torso precariously held aloft by spindly legs. Quizzical moon-round eyes staring at the oddities of the world from over an Uncle Willie cigar. Hair plastered flat on his head, and seersucker suit succumbing to the summer heat by early morning. The chubby fingers scribbling notes on folded newspaper copy paper with the surviving three inches of a #1 Herzog editing pencil. Retreating to a crude plank table in the press section, and his rickety Corona noiseless portable, to begin the day's story.

> PHILADELPHIA MENCKEN. The gallant Confederates who attempted a raid upon the late Democratic Convention got a bad licking. . . .

H.L. Mencken and American politics. He professed to detest the art ("a carnival of buncombe!") and the men who practiced it without even a passing nod at objectivity ("I am completely neutral. I'm against them all.") Yet for more than forty years Mencken lived a literary-journalistic double life. Whatever his business elsewhere, as respected editor and man of letters, each four years Mencken roared away to the political conventions, irresistibly drawn by a "spectacle as fascinating as a hanging, and often as grisly."

Writing in the era before television took *de facto* possession of the conventions, transforming them into living-room entertainment, Mencken made politics an acutely visual—and visceral—experience. Persons who read the *Baltimore Sun*, Mencken's primary outlet for politics, knew not only the color of the bunting on the hall but also the relative pulchritude of lady politicians of each party. (Not infrequently, he marveled, they resembled "British tramp steamers dressed for the King's birthday.") Mencken's concern was not so much what a man said, but how he performed: At the 1904 Republican convention, for instance, Congressman Joseph Cannon concluded his keynote speech "with a terrific avalanche of words and with a tremendous left swing that almost upset him . . . [F]or an old man, he stamped about with fine energy." Or, in 1932, describing President Herbert Hoover's oratorical style: "He is the sort of man who, if he had to recite the Twenty-third Psalm, would make it sound like a search warrant issued under the Volstead Act."

Mencken's political writing was *sui generis*, neither commentary nor reportage. Because he did his legwork, and because, whenever possible, he took care to sniff around a politician before writing about him, Mencken's analyses bore a special stamp of credibility. And the *Sun*'s headlines on his pieces indicate the editors recognized that Mencken was an integral part of the scene he described:

Mencken Calls Dixie
Chickens 'Spavined'

McAdoo a Corpse, But
To Mencken's Surprise
Won't Go in the Grave

Air of Deceit and Fraud
Pervades Whole G.O.P.
Meeting, Says Mencken

Professionals recognized Mencken's reporting energies as the wellspring of his talent: As a working journalist he would climb to the top rafters of the convention hall to secure the comments and plans of the bandmaster. He was often the only journalist, aside from the wire-service reporters, who would endure the droning banalities of platform committee hearings, muttering, "Bah bah bah," as he scrawled notes. Laymen, however, oft as not were attracted by a savagery of language seldom read in a serious American newspaper. After the Coolidge election in 1924 Mencken wrote, "The American people, having 35,717,342 native-born adult whites to choose from, including thousands who are handsome and many who are wise, pick out the Hon. Mr. Coolidge to be the head of state. It is as if a hungry man, set before a banquet prepared by master cooks, and covering a table an acre in area, should turn his back upon the feast and stay his stomach by catching and eating flies." (The *Methodist Review*, commenting upon this particular article, called Mencken a "slobbering street satyr" who had "adopted blackguardism as a profession, seeing in it his own best road to fortune.")

With his inventive command of the American language Mencken

could reduce a revered public figure to the ridiculous with a single sentence. (General Leonard Wood, a serious contender for the Republican presidential nomination in 1920, Mencken dismissed as "the simple-minded dragoon, viewing all human phenomena from the standpoint of the barracks-room.") Mencken's expertise at outrageous exaggeration meant he must be read with a cautiously cocked eyebrow; to take him at face value was to abandon credulity: yet his embellishments were never capricious; they satirically hit the political bull's eye. By matter-of-factly referring to Senator Robert M. La Follette as "the Wisconsin Red, with his pockets stuffed with Soviet gold," Mencken made a mockery of the charge that opponents actually were making against the senator.

Because they perform in public, their every utterance and gesture seen by a thousand onlookers, politicians were a species peculiarly vulnerable to Mencken. He detested hypocrisy, pomp, and delusions of high-mindedness—qualities endemic among office-seekers. Working from the premise that any candidate elected would do grave harm to the Republic, and common sense, Mencken covered politics not as a competitive sport but as a scramble between the "reigning clowns" and the "fourth-raters gaping at the swill-trough from afar." As he wrote in 1936, "Whatever the result of the plebiscite of November 3, we are in for four more years of grief and melancholy." Gloating over the Democrats' agony about Al Smith in 1928, when the South threatened to bolt rather than accept a Catholic nominee, Mencken had only backhanded praise for the pastime that provided him with such mirth:

> Has the art and mystery of politics no apparent utility? Does it appear to be unqualifiedly ratty, raffish, sordid, obscene and low down, and its salient virtuosi a gang of unmitigated scoundrels? Then let us not forget its high capacity to soothe and tickle the midriff, its incomparable services as a maker of entertainment.

For all his insight Mencken was capable of drastic miscalculations. During the 1924 Democratic convention, which stalemated for more than a hundred ballots, Mencken confidently pecked out a lead:

> Everything is uncertain in this convention but one thing: John W. Davis will never be nominated.

Informed a few minutes later that the convention had just swung to Davis, Mencken did not lose his aplomb. "Why, that's incredible! I've already sent off a story that it's impossible." A pause, then, "I wonder if those idiots in Baltimore will know enough to strike out the negative."

In 1924 Mencken had publicly declared support for the presidential candidacy of Senator La Follette, running on a third-party Progressive ticket: "He is the best man in the running . . . There is no ring in his nose . . . Suppose all Americans were like La Follette? What a country it would be! No more depressing goose-stepping. No more gorillas in hysterical herds. No more trimming and trembling . . ." But in 1936 his hatred of Franklin D. Roosevelt ("a vindictive fellow, despite his Christian Scientist smile") put him into lockstep with the Liberty League and other arch conservatives; he convinced himself that a "Chinaman could beat Roosevelt,"* renounced his standing as a "lifelong Democrat," and announced he intended to vote for Alfred Landon. Mencken's old friend, columnist Westbrook Pegler, marveled at finding "Old Henry Mencken gone Republican and gibbering in unknown tongues." Pegler steeled himself against the day when Mencken "joins the Tennessee fundamentalists and is totally immersed in Goose Crick wearing a white shirt and blubbering 'Hallelujah, Brother,' between plunges in the cleansing flood."

Mencken's exposure to national politics had begun in 1904, when the *Baltimore Herald* dispatched him to the conventions of both parties. Although only twenty-three, Mencken was already a seasoned newspaperman, and he relied upon basic reportorial skills to handle the assignment. Mencken's very first convention coverage contained elements that were to be his hallmarks in the next four decades—sufficient description to permit the reader to visualize the arena, capsule portraits of the leading figures, frequent hints that the spectacle is more than a little ridiculous—all written with awesome energy. (The 1904 articles ran as long as three and a half columns of six-point type). Mencken's first piece began:

> *From the Staff Correspondent of* The Herald
> Chicago, June 18—Chicago forgot the Republican national convention today and turned her back upon the incoming hordes of delegates, alternates, favored sons, shouters, boomers and musicians, for it was Derby day, and on Derby day Chicago goes to Washington Park track and sees fast horses run a mile and a half for $30,000. . . .

---

*Mencken later was to claim misinterpretation: "What I actually said was that if Roosevelt could be beaten at all, a Chinaman could do the job. The idea, of course, was that the vote would not be for his opponent, but against himself. The libel pops up regularly, and leads me to the despairing conclusion that journalism is not yet an exact science."

> When the Hawaiian delegation came in this morning . . . the people in the street, seeing the name of the balmy islands on a large blue banner, craned their necks for a sight of a black prince in native garb. When they saw three commonplace white men, who smoked cigars nonchalantly, and might have been from Bowie, Maryland, or Jackson, Mississippi, they went on about their business . . .

A month later Mencken trailed the Democrats to St. Louis and found them a more relaxed crowd, if not especially admirable.

> At Chicago the hullabaloo in the auditorium lobby was made by dignified gentlemen smoking genuine ten-center cigars, and about the walls gazing upon them sat handsome women in flashy silks and diamonds. Here the shouts come from the throats of men wearing slouch hats and enormous badges who spit on the floor and rush toward the bar with shrill, despairing cries and in flying wedge formation. At Chicago, the principal boomers donned dress suits at six o'clock, and despite the shadowy and oppressive fringe of colored brethren without, tried to look like the well-fed drove that inhabits the Waldorf-Astoria. Here the "boys" are of the gunpowder and blood school, and their drink comes from the bottle, undented by seltzer and lemon.

Two years later Mencken shifted from the *Herald* to the *Baltimore Sun*, commencing an association that was to continue, to one degree or another, until 1948. For the *Sun*, Mencken was variously Sunday editor, columnist (his "Monday columns" were a renowned institution of American journalism), and occasional specialist in "political, homiletical and patrio-inspirational orgies." (An example of the latter was the Scopes monkey trial, where Mencken's savaging of William Jennings Bryan, hired as special prosecutor to debunk Darwin's theory of evolution, demolished what shreds remained of that man's reputation.) The *Sun* was one career. Another role was that of editor, first of the *Smart Set* and then *The American Mercury*, the latter the most influential iconoclastic journal in the country from 1924 until HLM resigned in 1933. Yet another life was that of writer: Counting anthologies, Mencken ground out twenty-four books and a veritable torrent of articles on literature, language, manners, women, prohibition, and religion; by his own estimate, some 5 million "more or less serious words" appeared under his name during his lifetime.

But Mencken's audience stopped laughing along with him beginning in the mid-1930s, when he insisted on treating Hitler as little more than a harmless jackass, of the same genre as any number of American politicians. In an *American Mercury* editorial he even argued that Hitler's case "is often sensible enough," and his views on Jews hardly surprising because the "disadvantage of the Jew is that, to simple men, he often seems a kind of foreigner . . . Many of the current Jewish leaders in this country are very loud and brassy fellows." After reportorial trips to Germany Mencken concluded that the "Hitler New Deal" was working better than Roosevelt's.

As World War II approached, Mencken accepted the inevitable. His German heritage made him suspect, and his style made it impossible to "deal with quacks without handling them roughly." Knowing that commentary on current events would be impossible, he stopped writing for the *Sun* in October 1941 and turned to non-controversial work: a continuation of his memoirs, published first as sketches in *The New Yorker*, then in book form as *Happy Days, Newspaper Days*, and *Heathen Days; A New Dictionary of Quotations,* compiled both from scholarly sources and Mencken's rich imagination; and a sixteen-volume compilation of typescripts and other documents on his career as editor and writer.

By the time peace returned, Mencken was beginning a slow climb back to public acceptability, so much so that by August 1946 *Life* found him worthy of a formal profile. For that weekly Mencken spouted opinions and solutions for hours. He even knew what to do about John L. Lewis, the hirsute president of the United Mine Workers, whose strikes were an annual rite in the postwar years: "I suggested that the FBI kidnap him some dark night and shave off his eyebrows. It would have finished him." The interviewer, Roger Butterfield, finally asked in exasperation, "Mr. Mencken, which would you rather be called, 'The Sage of Baltimore' or 'The Man Who Hates Everything'?"

"I don't care a damn what you or anyone else calls me," Mencken answered, "just so long as you don't call me an old dodo sneaked out of the dissecting room. In the present case it is a little inaccurate to say that I hate everything. I am strongly in favor of common sense, common honesty, and common decency. This makes me forever ineligible to any public office of trust or profit in the Republic."

Around the same time James Daniels, of the Scripps-Howard newspapers, set out to answer the question, "Whatever happened to Henry L. Mencken?" and found stores reporting a revival of interest in Mencken's books. Although he was "not yet the rage of campus intellectuals as he was a generation ago when copies of *The American Mercury* were more plentiful in dormitories than raccoon coats or hip flasks," Daniels wrote, "there is something in the air of this second post-war period—a growth of skepticism and pessimism—which has renewed the appeal of the sage of Baltimore."

Physically, however, time was running out for Mencken, and most rapidly. Always a keen, if at times comically hypochondriac, student of his own body, Mencken found he could no longer summon the energy to sustain him through twelve hours at the typewriter. He had suffered a mild stroke in the summer of 1939, and his doctors thereafter constantly warned him he must slacken his pace or risk a killing seizure. Mencken tried, but a medical journal he kept beginning in 1940 reflects a seemingly unshakable morbidity. Mencken worried about his heart, his always-sensitive throat and sinuses, his familial proclivity toward strokes. (He had already outlived most of his male ancestors.) He was even concerned, in 1945, about losing his mental prowess, complaining of nervousness and confusion when he tried to write. In August 1947 another stroke, this one more serious, left him unable to sign his name, much less type or write, for several weeks. Each siege of illness sapped Mencken's morale and left him acutely aware that his productive days were rapidly drawing to a close; in one letter he complained he was "oxidizing." So much work to be done, he groused, so many projects that he wished to finish.

These did not include returning to the *Sun*. That was one old breach that was slow to heal. Mencken had never completely severed his ties, even when he stopped writing his column and giving editorial advice. He had remained both on the payroll (at $750 a month, as a consultant) and on the board of directors. Occasionally he suggested a feature article; he helped revise the style book, but when he came to the *Sun* to visit old friends the conversations tended to be stiff. He was an outsider, a position he didn't like. Mencken was sore: As a practical man he realized the *Sun* couldn't give space to a critic who wished to write of the war as an absurdity of civilization, in which the democracies behaved as knavishly as the fascists. Nonetheless, he felt he had been cast adrift by an institution to which he had devoted much of his professional life, and he constantly fretted to friends about the paper's pro-Roosevelt editorials.

After the war, as Mencken's popularity began to grow again, *Sun* executives realized that if they wanted him, they would have to court him. Some younger editorialists didn't think the old iconoclast was worth the bother. Mencken's virulent hatred of President Roosevelt*

*Already distrustful of Roosevelt as a potential tyrant, Mencken hated him personally after an episode at the 1934 Gridiron Club dinner in Washington. Mencken and FDR

and the New Deal had carried over to President Truman and most of the people around him, and the *Sun* was mildly pro-administration. He obviously did not march in step with the *Sun*'s policies. Why give space to a man who many on the staff considered to be an anachronistic eccentric?

But Paul Patterson, the *Sun* publisher, and Hamilton Owens, the principal editor, knew better. They recognized Mencken as a considerable journalistic asset for any newspaper, and they cautiously began strewing bait in Mencken's path, both in casual talks and in letters. As late as November 1947 Mencken was still saying no, but not in so firm a voice as before. Perhaps for reasons of pride, when Mencken finally made his decision, he chose to relay it to the *Sun* indirectly.

In an interview with the *New York Herald Tribune,* upon publication of the second supplement to his *The American Language*, Mencken declared he would cover the conventions: "I'm an old reporter and I can't stand by. I'll probably end up coming home on a shutter. Oh, well, it's a heroic death."

Maclean Patterson, Paul's son, excitedly wrote Mencken that the paper was reserving a press seat and a room for him at each convention, and told his father, "It looks as though Mr. Mencken is weakening!" But the *Sun* people continued to handle Mencken gingerly, renting an apartment in Rittenhouse Square, replete with butler and valet, for the *Sun* convention headquarters and assuring Mencken he would not have to do any writing unless he wished. Paul Patterson, of course, made this statement in full knowledge that Mencken would be constitutionally unable to sit idle amid his favorite spectacle. And so Mencken succumbed. "God knows I itch to see all three conventions," he told Maclean Patterson. Not that he expected much from the candidates nor of the electorate who would decide their fate. He thought all the politicians mentioned thus far "should be led out to a pasture and shot." In June he predicted that Truman would win, because "voters are boobs who distrust real intelligence and

---

were the main speakers, and the president, with wicked delight, used unidentified quotations from Mencken's essay, "Journalism in America," to roast the audience of correspondents. ("Most of the evils that continue to beset American journalism today, in truth, are not due to the rascality of owners nor even to the Kiwanian bombast of business managers, but simply and solely to the stupidity, cowardice and Philistinism of working newspapermen. The majority of them, in almost every American city, are still ignoramuses, and proud of it. . . .") Mencken felt he had been misused, and he never forgave FDR.

throw their caps for the candidate most closely approximating their collective IQs."

Thus was Mencken enticed back to the *Sun* and politics—a willing victim, to be sure, and one thrust back into action in a truly vintage year. Seldom had the American electoral scene been in such tumultuous, splendid disarray. The incumbent, Truman, staggered from crisis to crisis, the butt of many jokes ("Don't shoot the piano player, he's doing the best he can!" and "To err is Truman") and unable to command the respect of either the Democratic left or right. The Republicans, scenting victory for the first time in five elections, began with a field of seven serious contenders. But by convention time the primaries had winnowed the number to three: Governor Thomas E. Dewey of New York, the moderate-eastern favorite; Senator Robert A. Taft of Ohio, "Mr. Republican" to his party's conservative core; and Harold Stassen, elected governor of Minnesota in 1938 at age thirty-one and still youthful enough to be called a "boy wonder" by an occasional inexact journalist. (Mencken dismissed Stassen in the spring as a "western wind machine.") The trio bore old scars. At the 1940 convention Stassen had managed to double-cross both Dewey and Taft, to whom he had promised support, by a sudden bolt to Wendell Willkie. Although Republicans respected Taft's intellect, too many of them had felt the sting of his tart tongue to really like him. ("The senator is talking tommyrot," he once snapped to a GOP colleague during a floor debate.)

Dewey suffered personality problems of his own. Vain, priggish, disdainful of persons he considered inferior (that is to say, most people he met) Dewey had what journalist John Gunther called "one of the least seductive personalities in public life." The wife of a Republican leader in New York once said of him, "You have to know Dewey really well to dislike him." The public, however, knew Dewey chiefly as a racket-busting district attorney and as a progressive governor who managed to cut taxes in his first term and still maintain a $623 million surplus. Republican regulars might detest Dewey, but the man would win votes, and the party was ready to swallow whatever amount of bile necessary to gain the presidency.

Such was the scene when Mencken embarked for Philadelphia and the Republican convention early on Sunday, June 18, pausing to write a brief note to his friend Siegfried Weisberg, proprietor of Baltimore's Peabody Book Store: "I am off to Philadelphia in an hour. Such patriotic outpourings always fascinate me. I delight in seeing men sacrifice so much for God and country." Mencken declined the *Sun's* offer of lodging in the Rittenhouse Square quarters and camped instead in a hotel with Westbrook Pegler. Then he hurried across the Schuylkill to inspect the arena.

The mechanics of staging a convention always fascinated Mencken, and he spent the afternoon talking with sound engineers, guards, and floor staff—in a process peculiarly akin to a cat's sniffing through a strange house where he is to board awhile; Mencken felt more comfortable when he was sure of the layout of his surroundings.

The other reporters, of course, lost no time finding him, for his reappearance was a news event in itself. Mencken obliged them. Cigar wagging, he snapped out "predictions" of what was likely to happen. Personally, he wanted Herbert Hoover and Alfred Landon on the ticket. "Hoover is the buggy, and Landon the horse," he said. An interviewer, Hal Boyle of the Associated Press, protested this was putting the cart before the horse. "Not a bad idea," Mencken replied. The only adjustment he would entertain was the substitution of James A. Garfield for Hoover. Then he paused, "But wait a minute, is Mr. Garfield still living?" No, someone replied. "Well, that would be a handicap," Mencken conceded. Momentarily serious, Mencken found a compliment for Tom Dewey, whose spoken English he described as the best "of any man in public life today." And Mencken made an unconvincing pretense at not being all that excited about returning to political writing. "These conventions are all the same," he said. "They don't vary by one per cent. All bla-a-ah."

Unfortunately, Mencken didn't survive the Republican preliminaries. His first three pieces, devoted almost entirely to preparations for the convention, gave only a passing nod to contenders for the nomination. The logistics were awful enough. When the television networks tested their 10,000-watt lights the afternoon before the convention opened, Mencken basked a few moments in the pleasant warmth, then fled for the press bar, there to make "the rest of my observations . . . through a brown beer bottle."

On opening night Mencken finally got down to serious business, watching the keynote speaker, Governor Dwight Green of Illinois. Most of Green's audience sat through his oratory "with the dumb, resigned air of cattle waiting in the stockyards." Even Mencken seemed relieved when Green finally drew some spirit from the mob: "The most earnest clapper-clawing . . . followed the hon. gentleman's solemn promise that the new Republican president, whoever he is, will clean out all the dubious characters who now hog places at the public trough, feasting upon the taxpayers' vitals and disgracing the human race. All these nefarious persons, he said, will get the gate."

Alas, with that article Mencken bade farewell to the Republicans. The combination of the ferocious Philadelphia heat ("very high humidity and lazy puffs of gummy wind from the mangrove swamps surrounding the city") and the chill of hotel air conditioning gravely assaulted Mencken's sinuses, and he hacked and wheezed all week and finally surrendered. His scrapbook of convention articles contains the scrawl, "I fell ill on June 22, and had to come home, thus missing the rest of the convention. HLM." Writing to Siegfried Weisberg a few days later he blamed the air conditioning and diagnosed his ailment as tracheitis. But he was recuperating and promised to be ready for the Democratic convention: "It promises to be a lulu." Meanwhile, back in Philadelphia Dewey won on the third ballot, and Walter Lippmann wrote, "The problem is not how to beat Truman, but how to preserve the victory beyond 1948."

Truman's problems were real indeed, even within his own party. New Dealers saw him as a corrupter of the Rooseveltian ideal, a ward politician who could bumble the nation into war or economic chaos. Southern conservatives detested him because, unlike Roosevelt, he seemed serious about civil rights. Confronted by a series of grisly post-war lynchings of southern blacks, many of them veterans, that meant the national conscience could no longer ignore Dixie's treatment of Negroes, Truman sent a broad civil-rights message to Congress in January 1948, asking an end to the poll tax, a federal law against lynching, and a permanent Fair Employment Practices Commission. Southern politicians fell over themselves with alarm, accusing Truman of establishing "An American OGPU" and paying more attention to Harlem "than the entire white South." With a great flapping of their frock coats the southerners threatened to bolt the Democrats and run their own candidate. Truman didn't flinch.

On the left, Truman faced an uncertain insurgency led by an avowed enemy, former Vice-President Henry Wallace, who had been mad since Roosevelt dumped him in 1944. Wallace grudgingly stayed in Washington as secretary of commerce but behaved as if he bore more legitimate claim to the Roosevelt heritage than did Truman. The inevitable explosion came in September 1947, when Wallace used the forum of a Communist-tainted rally to attack "British imperialism"—at a time of intense Big Four negotiations over the future of postwar Europe. Worse, Wallace claimed Truman had blessed the speech.

Truman fired him, and Wallace marched out of the Democratic party with a call for a "Gideon's army" to assemble behind him to work for a "century of the common man."

On another front, many big-name Democrats, including two of the late President Roosevelt's sons, tried to persuade the vastly popular General Dwight D. Eisenhower, World War II hero of the European theater, to wrest the nomination from Truman. So did the leadership of the Congress of Industrial Organizations and Americans for Democratic Action. But Ike tenaciously refused to get into politics, either for the Democrats or the Republicans, and the draft boom faded. Truman methodically gathered the delegates necessary for nomination; his sole worry at the convention would be the Dixiecrat rebellion.

The Dixiecrat-Truman confrontation provided special sport for Mencken, because it gave prominence to his old adversary, the South. Mencken could not take the South seriously. To him, it epitomized the flaws of American democracy about which he had long complained—pillorying of freedom by an ignorant but powerful majority; an antipathy to literature and serious music; a disdain for civil liberties. Mencken could drink with Alabama Klansmen (as he did at the 1924 convention); he could even find a southern woman civilized enough to marry (Sara Haardt, who had died in 1935). But Mencken watched the "sub-Potomac politicos" with contempt: "The species . . . is excessively bellicose and even bloodthirsty, and there has not been a Democratic convention in history in which it did not stage a gory bout."

Mencken likened the southern dissidents descending upon Philadelphia to an invading army, replete with spies and advance detachments. And to his delight Truman's behavior on the civil-rights issue was a renewed demonstration of the dictum that a politician is *ipso facto* a weaseler or a liar. Having vowed to work for a strong civil-rights program, Truman had second thoughts the deeper he got into the election year. Hence, the platform committee, at the direction of the White House, repeated the generalities of the 1944 platform, rather than calling for passage of Truman's program. Only when liberals, led by Hubert H. Humphrey, the young mayor of Minneapolis, and Andrew Biemiller, a former Socialist congressman from Milwaukee, fought it out on the convention floor was a tougher plan inserted. Delegates from four southern states stormed out, charging betrayal. Three days later they regrouped in Birmingham and nominated Strom Thurmond, the governor of South Carolina, for president and Fielding Wright, governor of Mississippi, as his running mate.*

The Democratic convention was grinding work for Mencken. He would begin filing copy for the morning *Sun* early each afternoon, beginning with "end matter" to be incorporated deep into the body of the story. Then toiling at Convention Hall until far past midnight, he wrote a running description that was telegraphed to Baltimore seriatim, composing the lead paragraphs just before deadline. At the session at which Truman was nominated Mencken wrote upward of 8,000 words, including different leads for early editions of the *Sun*, and then a final revision that included an account of Truman's acceptance speech, which did not begin until half-past one in the morning.

Mencken began with material that ultimately became the twentieth paragraph of the final story, telegraphed to Baltimore with a note for the guidance of copy editors:

> (end mencken, to follow night lead to come)
>
> The walkout of the Alabamians was carried out quietly. Their state, as everyone knows, leads the alphabetical roll of states. When it was called . . .

This portion continued for fifteen paragraphs, about 750 words, ending:

> On the floor the lady politicos powdered their shiny noses and gritted their teeth. And so it went to the dreary end.

Mencken's next file was more complex:

> (Mencken to run after end matter sent this afternoon lead to come)
>
> The afternoon session was adjourned to 6:30 P.M., but it was 7 o'clock before Chairman Rayburn clouted the convention to something resembling order. . . .

And, finally, after midnight, a first lead, marked

> (Lead mencken, to run ahead of end matter)
>
> by H.L. Mencken
> Convention Bureau of the Sun
>
> Philadelphia, *Thursday,* July 15. President Truman was duly nominated early this morning by the Democrats in convention

---

*Dead-tired after eight days with the Democrats, Mencken let the Dixiecrats fend for themselves.

> assembled. The business passed off smoothly and peacefully, to the tune of immense cataracts and bad oratory. . . .

But Mencken's work was not yet done. Several hours later he filed a final lead, to run atop a story that incorporated much but not all of what he had written during the session.

> Philadelphia, *Thursday*, July 15. It was half past one this morning before President Truman got to the platform of the Democratic National Convention to accept the nomination, though he had been stored away in another part of the hall, surrounded by his family, his friends, and a large force of Secret Service men, for hours. . . .

Mechanically, writing a "running" convention story—in effect, describing an event while it is in progress—is one of the more difficult journalistic feats, for the reporter must be mindful of the clock, of what he has already filed, and of what is apt to happen. Press tables are invariably cramped and cluttered, with elbows and carbons overlapping, the roar of the crowd a constant echo, and the glare of arc lights an ophthalmological insult. Some writers can perform in such circumstances; others cannot. Mencken loved it. His British friend Alistair Cooke, who watched him work at Philadelphia, marveled at "that deliberate manual incompetence which is one of the professional reporter's occupational vanities." Cooke continued:

> Mencken carried it to the extreme of parody, hitting the keys only with his two stubby forefingers and spacing with his elbow, like a stud horse imitating a drum majorette. He would gaze in a steady trance at the keyboard, while the loudspeakers rattled with the sobs and bawlings of the party chieftains. . . .

Despite these chaotic conditions, Mencken's convention stories are typed virtually letter-perfect. The occasional changes (witness the carbon copies he saved in scrapbooks now in the Enoch Pratt Free Library) add a barb to a sentence or change a phrase from the mundane to the Menckenesque. Cardinal Dougherty of Philadelphia, the first time out of Mencken's typewriter, simply "waited for the mike." Then a line of XXXXXXX through the phrase; he now "waited with archiepiscopal fortitude for the mike." Similarly referring to the Progressive candidate merely as "Wallace" does not suffice. A tap-tap-tap of the X key, and he is "the Swami Wallace."

In addition to his own work, a considerable volume, Mencken did what he could to assist his *Sun* colleagues charged with straightforward convention reporting. William H. Y. Knighton, of the *Sun*'s

Washington bureau, recollected, "There was no air conditioning in the convention hall, and my most vivid memory of the conventions is of Henry soaking wet with sweat, so much so that his entire suit dripped water, sitting and pounding away at his typewriter. The heat and discomfort didn't slow him down a damned bit, although he was an older fellow. And he was a good man to have in the [convention] bureau. He didn't do the straight coverage, of course, his main concern was the columns. But when he got his hands on hard news—as he did, because he was all over the convention, listening to everyone—he made certain he passed it on to someone doing the main story. He was a handy guy to have."

Another *Sun* colleague, Paul Y. Ward, wasn't so sure. Ward felt Paul Patterson wanted Mencken at the conventions for reasons of personal ego as much as for what he could contribute to the paper. "Mencken attracted celebrities like fresh meat draws flies," Ward said. "Everyone gathered around the *Sun* bureau and the *Sun* hospitality suite to talk with him. Patterson never went to another convention after 1948—no reason to, Mencken wasn't there." And some of the regular political reporters from Washington viewed Mencken's return with skepticism. Marquis Childs, long of the *St. Louis Post-Dispatch* (and a man who had been friendly with Mencken and written for *The American Mercury*), felt that "Mencken was so fixed in his views, especially on Roosevelt and any Democrat who followed him, that it was hard for a working journalist to consider him a serious political reporter. Mencken was frozen into a reactionary, anti-New Deal attitude."

For reporters from elsewhere, however, Mencken remained a garrulous folk hero, a man always ready with a pithy quote when they came around for interviews, knowing, as a professional, the value that an outrageous statement adds to a feature story. Chatting with George Dixon, of the *New York Daily News*, Mencken declared, "Everybody named Henry should be put to death. If somebody will do it for Henry Wallace, I promise to commit suicide." Watching the Progressives with Earl Wilson, of the *New York Post*, he shook his head and exclaimed, "I have never heard worse speeches on this earth, nor seen more hideous lady politicians." At one point Mencken encountered an old acquaintance, Norman Thomas, the perennial Socialist candidate for president—a man he liked personally even if he thought his politics foolish. Mencken and Thomas began recalling past conventions, and they agreed the best speech they had ever heard was by the Reverend Gerald L. K. Smith, a noisy old bigot associated with many of the nut causes in America during the 1930s and 1940s. By

Mencken's memory, even cynical reporters were clapping and cheering when Smith finished, though only he could call up a specific line: "The pigs that Henry Wallace killed out in Iowa* caused the death by starvation of 200,000 children, born and unborn, in the Carolinas alone." Lewis Nordyke, of the Amarillo, Texas, *News*, who listened to the two old men reminisce, wrote later:

> Mencken has been a fighter. But he's mellow now. . . . He says he's had a good time and that he's happy about the life he has lived and the work he has accomplished. He realizes his era has passed. He is still one of the best reporters in the business.

As a connoisseur Mencken expected the Wallace convention "to be an obscenity in the grand manner," and the Progressives did not disappoint him. After an encouraging start the Wallace campaign had taken on heavy encrustations of Communists and fellow-travelers, to the dismay of non-Marxist liberals who had hoped for a viable progressive alternative to Truman. The respectable left dropped away from Wallace in chunks, leaving him almost totally dependent on an inner core of Communists as his advisers. Wallace refused to repudiate their support, and much of his convention machinery was directed by Lee Pressman, the former CIO general counsel who later admitted he was a Communist. Further, Wallace attracted an across-the-board sampling of classic American eccentrics ranging from single-taxers to amateur metaphysicians to health faddists.

"People who enjoy visiting zoos should never miss the opportunity to inspect the animals at first hand," Mencken said soon after arriving for the Progressive fete, and so he was off to Wallace's hotel suite for a chat with the candidate and his wife. They exchanged pleasantries, and Wallace invited the photographers in to take pictures of him and Mencken arm in arm. The conviviality was short-lived; within an hour Wallace and Mencken were in tense confrontation in one of the convention's livelier moments. The difficulty had to do with the so-called guru letters:

As secretary of agriculture, Wallace had become fascinated with a Russian mystic named Nicholas Konstantinovich Roerich, guru of a sect of theosophists. Well-known in offbeat religious circles, if not respected by conventional theologians, Roerich developed a following that included such relative luminaries as the composer Igor Stravinsky. In 1934 Wallace put Roerich on the federal payroll and

---

*As secretary of agriculture in the early New Deal, Wallace sought to boost farm prices through production controls, a scheme that included the slaughter of piglets.

dispatched him to Outer Mongolia. The exact job he was to perform was murky, but Wallace claimed that Roerich was to search out a strain of drought-resistant grass for the dust-bowl states. Some of Wallace's colleagues later maintained the grass story was a cover—that Roerich had convinced Wallace he could find evidence of the imminent Second Coming of Christ. Whatever the true reason, Wallace and Roerich fell out, and the secretary dismissed the guru from federal service.

There matters rested until 1940, when Wallace was running for vice-president. Someone slipped the Republican National Committee a stack of letters that Wallace supposedly had written to Roerich during their friendship. By the most charitable interpretation the letters were nonsensical. The writer addressed Roerich as "Dear Guru" and the letters contained a plethora of code names for famous persons. President Roosevelt, for instance, was "the Flaming One," and Winston Churchill "the Roaring Lion." Cordell Hull, the dour secretary of state, appropriately was called "the Sour One." The writer told of curing himself of headaches at formal dinners by rubbing a Tibetan amulet on his forehead. A typical passage read:

> I have been thinking of you holding the casket—the sacred, most precious casket. And I have thought of the new country going forth, to meet the seven stars under the sign of the three stars. And I have thought of the admonition, "Await the stones."

Some of the letters were signed "Wallace," others, "Galahad."

Unable to establish the letters' authenticity beyond a doubt (Wallace denied authorship) and unnerved by a Democratic counter-threat to expose a love affair of Wendell Willkie's, the Republicans decided not to use them. In 1947, however, Westbrook Pegler got his hands on the letters, accepted them as real, and wrote a savage series of columns challenging Wallace's sanity. He demanded that the candidate reveal whether he still regarded Roerich "as a god or supernatural master of mankind as many of your associates in the cult did." But Pegler could not get Wallace to comment. Although he had not been covering the Progressive convention (lacking a congenial roommate, Mencken finally moved into the *Sun*'s apartment), Pegler traveled to Philadelphia to beard Wallace at a press conference.

Wallace flushed at the sight of Pegler, but called on the reporter and was asked point blank whether he wrote the letters. His voice tight, Wallace responded, "I do not answer questions put to me by Westbrook Pegler." When Martin Hayden of the *Detroit News* asked the same question, Wallace said, "I don't answer questions put to me by a stooge of Westbrook Pegler, either."

Then Mencken arose. "Mr. Wallace, do you consider me a stooge of Westbrook Pegler?" The assemblage laughed, and Wallace managed a smile.

"No, Mr. Mencken," he said, "I would never consider you anybody's stooge." (Pegler wrote later, "Mencken, being an atheist, was ready to swear on the Baltimore city directory that he put only his own questions.")

"Well, then," Mencken continued, "it is a simple question. We have all written love-letters in our youth that would bring a blush later on. This is a question that everyone here would like to have answered, so we can move on to weightier things."

Wallace held firm. "I will never engage in any discussion whatsoever with Westbrook Pegler," he said.

"But what about the letters?" Mencken pressed. Wallace again refused. Doris Fleeson said Mencken's questions came "in the most paternal and kindly manner . . . [He] sought to relieve the ugly tension."

But Wallace would not listen: "I will handle that matter in my own way, at my own time, and not here," he said.

"Answer the question," Mencken urged him, politely. "Say yes or no and be done with it. It can't hurt you . . . Why not answer now? We are all here."

Wallace supporters began shouting at the reporters to move to another subject, one of them yelling, "If you stooges don't like this, why don't you get out of here?" They did; in a trice the hall emptied of all reporters save those from Communist publications.

The press hitherto had ignored the guru letters. But the news conference put the subject onto the nation's front pages, driving the final nails into the coffin bearing Wallace's candidacy.

So far as Mencken was concerned, Wallace's "imbecile handling" of the guru matter cost him and his followers any future claim to even tolerable respect. The guru episode, Mencken wrote the next day, "made no more impression on his communicants than if it had been discovered that he had found a nickel on the street or joined the Tall Cedars of Lebanon." In his followers' eyes Wallace had "acquired the semi-celestial characteristics of the late FDR. If, when he is nominated today, he suddenly sprouts wings and begins flapping about the hall, no one will be surprised." Turning to Wallace's running mate, Senator Glen H. Taylor of Idaho, a onetime singing cowboy, Mencken wrote:

> Soak a radio clown for ten days and ten nights in the rectified juices of all the cow-state Messiahs ever heard of, and you have him to the life. Save on the remotest fringes of the intellectually underprivileged it is highly unlikely that he will add anything to the strength of the new party.

The press and the politicians had read Mencken avidly during the first two conventions—the *Sun* outsold even the local papers in the Philadelphia hotels—and concluded that his old bite was not quite there. Now, however, Mencken was back in prime condition, and Wallace heard the deadly guffaws of laughter as his convention played out its last dreary hours. According to one journalist, "One evening I saw no less than six of the best political writers in America leaning over a guy's shoulder at the press table, roaring with laughter as they read Mencken on Wallace. He sat off to the side writing—beaming as if he was the little boy who had played an especially nasty trick on the teacher."

The Progressive rank and file turned on Mencken with cold fury (even though many delegates did not recognize him in the flesh, and responded with smiles and waves when he addressed them in the hotel lobby as "Comrade"). In one piece Mencken praised a convention speaker but noted in passing he had "the complexion of a good ten-cent cigar." A claque of militants descended upon the press benches the next day, and stood over Mencken hissing and booing. The Maryland delegation even presented a formal resolution of censure against Mencken for "Hitlerite references to the people of this convention," claiming that he "Red-baits, Jew-baits and Negro-baits" and that "his obscenities against the American people mark him as unfit to report the proceedings of a people's convention . . . [T]herefore be resolved . . . that this convention severely censures H. L. Mencken and his contemptible rantings which pass for newspaper reporting."

Mencken sat at his typewriter and beamed: Not since the Arkansas legislature demanded his deportation in the 1920s had he been the subject of such official attention. He asked a Progressive functionary for an extra copy: "I'd like to have it notarized for deposit in my family archives." But the presiding officer refused to entertain the censure motion on grounds it would "start a flood of such denunciations against other reporters."

The night the convention ended, Mencken joined *Sun* colleagues for a festive farewell party in Paul Patterson's hotel suite. There was laughter, talk, and ample beer and sandwiches. Alistair Cooke, the only non-*Sun* man present, was struck by the way that Mencken "sat simply as an old reporter among equals." Long after midnight Wallaceite youths began racing through the hotel corridors, shouting imprecations at the "capitalist press," and chanting and singing. Soon five or six youths of the Minnesota Youth for Wallace brigade, banners unfurled, were in the *Sun* suite, demanding that the "capitalists" introduce themselves. Mencken passed Cooke off as a reporter from the London *Daily Worker*, made sure that the intruders got glasses of beer, and persuaded them to join him in singing a Wallace campaign song:

> Lumberjacks and teamsters
> And sailors from the sea;
> And there's farming boys from Texas
> And the hills of Tennessee;
> There's miners from Kentucky,
> And there's fishermen from Maine,
> All a-ridin' with us
> On this Wallace-Taylor train.

Mencken winced at the cadence but struggled through to the end. He lured the kids into a stanza of *The Star-Spangled Banner*, but when he demanded "the national anthem of Mr. Cooke," they grabbed their banners and bolted. Mencken sat down and laughed.

Mencken was not well as he rode the train home alone. He complained of dizziness, and his physicians counseled rest. Hence he decided not to attempt to travel with the candidates. But he did get to see a respectable smattering of them in the flesh in Baltimore campaign appearances: Strom Thurmond ("an elegant meeting, soft in tone, with no hint of demagogy"); Earl Warren, Dewey's running mate ("His voice is clear, but there is little resonance in it, and no one would call him an orator"); Norman Thomas ("a really intelligent and civilized man" whose speech was given "in a little L-shaped hall 45 steps up a steep stairway above a Chinese restaurant at 107 North Eutaw Street"); and Alben Barkley, the Democratic vice-presidential candidate ("a highly competent rabble-rouser").

To casual students of Mencken his most surprising pre-election column was a tacit declaration that the Dixiecrat case made much sense. Given Mencken's opinion of the South ("a sewer of imbecility . . . [that] has supported every major aberration, whether political or social, that has afflicted the country . . .") the column was ironic. Yet it was not hypocritical. Mencken abhorred segregation, but he had an even stronger aversion to the sweeping extensions of federal power that had commenced during the New Deal. He stood on common philosophical ground with southerners who opposed federal registrars for voters, federal laws against lynchings, and federal rules on hiring minorities. Writing a few weeks before the election, he argued that the Dixiecrats deserved serious attention, that they represented a movement transcending regional considerations. Many intelligent southerners, he maintained, "are painfully aware of what went on in the seventies, and they are naturally fearful of a repetition, with northerner jobholders, most of them dishonest and nearly all of them jackasses, substituted for the carpetbaggers of the first canto. They believe that they have some civil rights, too . . . I must confess that I sympathize with them, despite my life-long devotion to exposing their deficiencies."

Mencken felt so strongly about the Dixiecrat cause that he was prepared to vote for Thurmond, only to be denied the opportunity by the Maryland attorney general, who ruled the party off the ballot for technical reasons. So in the end he voted for Dewey, with extreme reluctance, and only because he felt the New Yorker to be plainly better than Truman. Mencken felt Dewey killed himself by not putting any real ideas in his speeches. From Truman he expected a "circus in the grand manner"; he considered Truman cunning but stupid and predicted that the quacks surrounding him would take charge. Why did Truman win? "If there were a formidable body of cannibals in the electorate last Tuesday, President Truman would have promised them American missionaries, fattened at the taxpayers' expense."

The election took place on November 2. A week later Mencken wrote his last newspaper column, a fierce attack on Baltimore officials for arresting a group of whites and blacks who played tennis together in a city park, in violation of a city ordinance against integrated sports. Mencken railed at the "spirit of the Georgia cracker surviving in the Maryland Free State and under official auspices . . . It is high time such relics of Ku Kluxery be wiped out in Maryland."

Two weeks later, on the evening of November 23, Mencken visited the apartment of his longtime secretary, Mrs. Rosalind Lohrfinck, to read through her day's typing. After they had chatted awhile, he complained of a headache. She gave him a drink, the glass slipped from his hand, he began to babble incoherently. For several days the doctors thought he would not survive the crippling stroke. He did, but without the faculties of reading, writing, and speaking that had been so much of his existence. He held onto life for more than seven years—his ability to comprehend what he heard ebbing and flowing, his spirits alternately glum and accepting. He tended to avoid old friends, for reasons sadly related by George C. Dorsch, a *Sun* editor and critic for forty-four years.

Dorsch stood in the foyer of the Lyric Theater in Baltimore one evening waiting to hear the Philadelphia Orchestra perform a program of Beethoven—one of the few composers who would attract Mencken to a formal concert. Dorsch saw his friend enter on the arm of another man, his gait slow and stumbling. "I knew he hadn't been feeling well, so I walked over to him. I said, 'Hello, Henry,' and moved to shake his hand. He looked at me with an absolute blank expression on his face. He had not the slightest idea who I was—and I had been among his closest friends. I murmured something and moved away. That was among the sadder moments of my life."

It ended for Mencken early the morning of January 29, 1956, in his sleep at home at age seventy-five.

I

The Republicans

Mencken Tunes In

Expects Blitz Of Sound From Heirs Of Lincoln

PHILADELPHIA, JUNE 18—The loudest bursts and blasts of sound ever heard on earth will greet the heirs of Lincoln when they assemble here on Monday to choose a David to butcher the pocket-size giant of Independence, Mo.

This, at all events, is what I gather from the uproar and hullabaloo on the part of engineers who have been swarming over the convention hall all day. They have rigged up a loud-speaker system that is to any loud-speaker system of the past as the range of the Himalayas is to a crabcake.

Turn up your radio to the highest point it will go, so that your walls shake, all the bottles fall off your cellar shelves, and your neighbors howl for the police. Well, the sound coming out of it will be only one eight hundredth as loud as that the heirs are booked for.

Prepare For Masterpiece

The prayers of the chaplain, as magnified, will drown out a choir of lions, and the sweetest, coyest remarks of the youngest and least hideous of stateswomen will match a series of boiler explosions.

All this I learn from the engineers in person. They have prepared for a masterpiece, and they are raring to go.

No less than twenty loud-speakers are already hanging from the ceiling, booked to an overhead rail system which permits them to be rushed from place to place as circumstances dictate, and on the platform are four supercolossal loud-speakers, each measuring a cubic yard, and all aimed at the hard chairs on which the delegates and alternates will sweat and suffer.

Nor will the shocks and reverberations of this infernal machinery be confined to the arena of statecraft.

There is a branch of it which will afflict and macerate what is hoped will be an overflow meeting in the exhibition hall downstairs.

There is another which will run into a banquet hall somewhere else in the huge building.

There is a third which may be turned upon any crowd or crowds that may be gathered outside. And there is a fourth which may be diverted, though with considerable toning down, into the common ducts of the national radio networks.

Many other marvelous things might be told of this incomparable loud-speaker system, but I have space to add but one. Every element of it, according to a hand-out issued by the engineers, may be operated independently.

Veteran Crowd Engineer Hired

That is to say, one may be set to shoot out the oratory on tap on the convention platform, another may transmit a colloquy on the floor between two delegates or two mobs of delegates, and a third may report a fist fight down in one of the washrooms.

Everyone expects this unprecedented hurricane of sound to heat up the delegates, the alternates and the spectators and in consequence elaborate preparations have been made to police them. To this end the national committee has hired a veteran crowd engineer from Chicago, by the name of Andy Frain.

Andy has been handling such things for 27 years, and for 17 of them he has kept order among the frenzied horse-lovers who frequent the Kentucky Derby. He knows how to calm and placate both big crowds and little crowds, but he is at his best when he tackles big ones, full of malicious animal magnetism.

Here in Philadelphia he has organized a force of shock troops that he is proud of, and expects to make a world's record. It is not made up of ward heelers and saloon loafers, as is commonly the case at national conventions, but of college men exclusively. All of them are close to six feet high and even the weakest can put the shot a hundred yards.

To Show Deference

He has outfitted them in neat blue uniform coats and instructed them to wear dark trousers, white shirts and blue or black neckties. They will bear no weapons save their own ham-like fists, and it is Professor Frain's hope that they will be forced to use even these only occasionally.

All day he has been instructing them in the principles of the art of which he is a master. Every one entering the hall will be approached politely and asked "may I help you, sir or madam?"

If the customer is a delegate or alternate he will be shown to his place as if he were an ambassador, and if he is so far in his cups that his legs tangle, two ushers will assist him, one on each side. If, later on, he falls out of his chair, he will be rushed to the first-aid station downstairs in a swift, silent and humane manner.

Professor Frain's instructions to his force of M.P.'s conclude as follows:

"No short-sleeved shirts or polo shirts will be allowed. Every usher must shave daily and see that his hair is trimmed. Do not slouch at your post. If you must smoke, do it out of public view. Our future president will be nominated in this hall."

Whether or not the last sentence will be eliminated when the Democrats and Wallace fans follow I do not know.

Hon. Mr. Bender On Scene

The only candidate so far seen on the actual fire ground has been the Hon. Riley Alvin Bender, a Chicago hotel keeper. He is distributing a circular which seems to show that he received 324,029 votes in the recent Republican primary in Illinois, as against 6,672 for General MacArthur, 1,572 for the Hon. Mr. Stassen, 953 for Governor Dewey and 705 for Senator Taft.

I asked the Hon. Mr. Bender today how he accounted for these strange returns. He said that the answer was easy. For one thing he had been in circulation for many months, haranguing the plain people in every village of Illinois. For another thing he was running on the platform that had everything and then some. All the usual planks are in it, and in addition, he promises to raise the income-tax exemption to $2,000 for bachelors and $4,000 for married men.

Also perhaps, there is the fact that Governor Dwight Green of Illinois refused to run in the primary, but gave over all his time and attention to preparing for his duties as temporary chairman of the convention. He is here now, practicing, and fully expects to wow them.

Mencken Listens—

But About All He Hears From GOP Is Vague Talk

PHILADELPHIA, JUNE 19—The traditional weather of a national convention began to clamp down upon Philadelphia last night. It started with a thunderstorm so vociferous that the sound seemed to be coming through the loud-speaker of the convention hall, and it continued today with a rising temperature, very high humidity, and lazy puffs of gummy wind from the mangrove swamps surrounding the city.

By Monday, if all goes well, the incoming delegates and alternates will begin their opening session in a high state of perspiration. Even today the early comers are breaking out their seersucker suits and sweatproof plastic collars, and the scenes in the hotels are taking on the aspect of a steamboat excursion.

Stassen As Prophet

Press conferences are being held by the candidates and their agents at intervals of a couple of hours, but little comes out of these affairs save vague and optimistic talk. The Hon. Harold Stassen today reiterated his prophecy that he will be nominated on the ninth ballot, but no one could pin him down to the precise mathematics of it.

The best he would offer was a fond recollection, to wit, that he had predicted in 1940 that the late Willkie would be nominated on the sixth ballot, and that it came out exactly so, with plus or minus allowance of less than one tenth of one per cent.

Equally Sure And Evasive

Governor Dewey's camerlingo, Brother Brownell* was equally sure and equally evasive. He said that delegates were drifting into his headquarters in a steady stream, to whisper that they were making

*Herbert Brownell, Dewey's campaign manager, and later attorney general in the Eisenhower administration.

ready to be had, but when he was asked who these delegates were and where they came from he let it pass.

After some sharp cross-examination, however, he admitted that most of them were from favorite-son states, and hence not pledged to any of the more salient candidates.

These press conferences are well attended and there lingers a hope among the newspaper correspondents that soon or late, if they are patient, something in the nature of news may turn up. So far it has not happened, save in the instance when Senator Vandenberg was propelled into the field of overt candidates. But there is no telling when either a candidate or an agent may let fall something of social significance.

Readying Dewey Reception

At the Dewey headquarters in the grand ballroom of the Bellevue Stratford Hotel, the day was mainly given to preparations for the grand reception planned for tomorrow, after the governor and his lady arrive from New York. This reception will be glorified and no doubt whooped up a little by a lavish outpouring of presents.

The Dewey agents insist that they have spent nothing whatever for these presents, but that every item is the freewill offering of some patriotic New York merchants.

They consist of makeup kits (four different kinds), slips, Nylon stockings, negligées, pocketbooks and even dresses. Every lady visitor, whether a delegate or not, will get something, and every hundredth comer will get a prize of a superswell worth.

At the start it was proposed to give this prize to every two hundredth visitor, and so many objects of beauty or utility began pouring in today that the ground rules were revised in haste.

New Yorkers' Privilege

No merchant save a New Yorker is permitted to cut in. Today a Philadelphia furrier offered a grand prize in the form of a sworn promise to keep the winner's furs clean and mothproof for life, but he was turned down. Also, the offer of a free slenderizing course by another Philadelphian was rejected, partly because it is considered gauche to mention tonnage to a lady politician and partly, as I have said, because entries are confined to New Yorkers.

This last condition is explained by the females in charge of the show on the ground that only a New Yorker can truly appreciate the vast services of Dewey to humanity.

This morning they bethought them of an oversight. Plenty of stockings, slips, negligées, etc., were on hand for the ladies, but what of their husbands left at home, maybe with babies to feed and lull to sleep or elder children to rescue from the police?

Hints Of Treachery

What indeed, of poor John, Fred and Otto, the desolate consorts of loud, brassy politicianesses?

To think was to act and now there are some nobby take-home gifts for these unfortunate creatures. There are cigarette holders for them, and not only cigarette holders, but also wallets, suitcases and ash trays. Finally, believe me or not, there are elegant boxes of candy.

All of the candidates and their agents are beginning to throw out hints that treachery is abroad. The Dewey people are extremely suspicious of Governor Stassen's recent stopover in Chicago, and the Stassen people, Taft and Vandenberg believe that the Dewey people are up to something nefarious.

It is probable that there is some truth in every one of these surmises for we are coming close to the final struggle and when it is reached no hold will be barred.

Mencken's Bottlescope

Television Lamps Stir Up 2-Way Use For Beer

PHILADELPHIA, JUNE 20—Television will take its first real bite at the statesmen of America tomorrow, and this afternoon there was a sort of experimental gumming or rehearsal in Convention Hall.

It passed off well enough, all things considered, and no one was actually fried to death.

But I doubt if any politician, however leathery his hide, survives that unprecedented glare of light without a considerable singeing. I was sitting quietly in the almost empty press-stand when the first 10,000-watt lamp was turned on.

Through A Brown Beer Bottle

The initial sensation was rather pleasant than otherwise, for it was a good deal like that of lolling on a Florida beach in midsummer. But in a few minutes I began to wilt and go blind, so the rest of my observations had to be made from a distance and through a brown beer bottle.

Of these 10,000-watt lamps there are ten in the galleries, all focused on the speakers' stand. And a little above and directly in the front of the stand there is a cluster of ten more, though each of these rates but 5,000 watts.

Newsreel Lights Now Easy

Once during the afternoon the whole battery was in action at once. The effect was very little less than that of an atomic bomb. The few hard-boiled fellows who faced it out on the platform began by looking almost transparent, and then showed a phosphorescent glow. The hardiest stood it only a few minutes.

How often this whole battery will be turned on I do not know. Today, fortunately, most of it was usually dark, for the business before the House was a rehearsal for the newsreels, not for television.

I recall the day when the newsreel lights were frightening, but now they seem like small potatoes. Every politician of any experience faces them bravely. But what the television lights will do to these same great patriots tomorrow remains to be determined.

The ladies who will cavort before them are running about town tonight seeking advice about television makeup. The report circulates that it differs enormously from makeup for the movies, for the newsreels, or even for stoking a blast furnace.

Grease-Paint Research

One female politico told me that she had learned that all the ordinary pigments were ineffective, and that it would be necessary to lay in purple, green and even black grease paints. Inasmuch as it was Sunday, no theatrical supply house was open, and the poor girls had to postpone their inquiries until tomorrow morning.

The star of the newsreel performance was the Hon. Dwight H. Green, governor of Illinois, who will be the keynoter.

He appeared in a neat double-breasted blue suit, a checkered white-and-black necktie and shoes with white tops, and wore a gilt badge with six bars. He is of about the stature and bulk of President Truman, but like Truman is a pert and lively fellow, and so he made an excellent impression upon the newsreel boys.

Posing And Intoning

First they posed him shaking hands with the Hon. Walter S. Hallanan, chairman of the committee on arrangements of the Republican National Committee; then they posed him shaking hands with the Hon. Carroll Reece, chairman of the national committee, and then they posed him waving his arm at the empty benches.

So much done, they put him to intoning his speech, after first sending a man to the mike to warn a few persons present that what he said was not to be revealed until his actual speech began tomorrow night.

All of this hocus-pocus was necessary because the newsreel boys know by bitter experience that during the delivery of this actual speech it will be difficult to mug him, what with the crowding in the aisles, the inevitable breaking-down of the lighting system, and other such hazards.

Precanned Keynote

The pictures made today went to New York at once, and there

they will be developed and printed tonight, and the prints packed in cans.

These cans will go out by air to hundreds and perhaps even thousands of movie parlors, and tomorrow evening at the precise moment the hon. gentleman bursts into his first sentence, they will begin to unroll, and while he roars on, movie audiences from Omaha to Atlanta will follow him yell for yell and blow for blow.

His whole speech, of course, will not be sent out, but only its more palpitating moments.

Two Tries For Reece

I violate no confidence when I tell you that there will be plenty of them, and that every enemy of the American way of life on earth, from Stalin to Truman, will get a severe mauling.

The Hon. Mr. Hallanan was also mugged today and likewise the Hon. Mr. Reece.

Reece blew up in the fourth sentence of his speech calling the convention to order, but it made no difference to the newsreel boys, for they simply ordered him to go back to the start and do it again. This time he was letter-perfect, but as an added precaution they made him do it twice more.

The whole business went on with the halts and stumbles of a wedding rehearsal in a church. When all was ready for the start someone discovered that there was no gavel on the platform, so there was a long delay until one was found in the basement.

Some Very Free Sweating

Even under the mild newsreel lights Reece did some very free sweating.

Tomorrow, under the television superglare, he may faint or even catch fire. But no one is worried about that, for the national committee has a blanket accident policy on all participants in the convention, with a very juicy indemnity for the widow of any who is actually put to death.

The decorations of the hall were completed tonight, and it is ready for the opening orgies tomorrow morning.

The city of Philadelphia some time ago spent a lot of money having it repainted, and it is now rather charming in its color scheme, with thin blue lines relieving flat surfaces of a sightly yellow, and high points of gilt here and there.

Too Simple For Politicians

But politicians cannot endure such simple effects, which strike them as fit only for churches and tearooms. In order to enjoy a homey feeling they have twined the galleries, the platform and the high shelves which bear the television and movie lights with streamers of red, white and blue bunting, apparently borrowed from a street carnival.

Along the front of the platform they have set a row of seven gilded eagles, and linking the eagles are festoons of gilded oak leaves. Directly in front of the speakers' stand is a spray of gladiolas larger than any ever seen at a funeral since that of John L. Sullivan.

A small portrait of Abraham Lincoln hangs from the proscenium arch above the platform.

Cushions For Committee Only

The seats on which the delegates and alternates will suffer appear to be upholstered, but this is mainly an optical delusion, as the occupants will quickly discover. The upholstery is actually wafer-thin, and the hardwood below will come into action with little amelioration.

The only chairs in the hall that are really cushioned are those reserved for the members of the national committee. Their seats and backs have thick pads filled with steel wool, and their arms and legs are of gas-pipe plated with chrome. The seats in the press-stand and galleries have no upholstery at all.

The markers indicating the places of the different state delegations, traditionally made by nailing crude cardboard signs to broomsticks, are of white on black plastic, with pink borders, and metal standards.

The standards fit into clasps at the floor-level, and may be removed without any unseemly tugging and cussing whenever there is a parade.

Unhappily, getting them back when the parade is over will be something else again. It is thus very probable that they will wander, as usual, to far places, and that Marylanders may end the proceedings as Hawaiians and honest Georgians as fiends in human form from New Hampshire or Vermont.

The television brethren are not only encroaching on the newsreel boys, but also on the radio boys. There was a time when the latter occupied all of a long glass-enclosed perch high up on the wall behind the platform. But now the television brethren have got a lodgement in this perch. Indeed, they are already hogging both ends of it, and the poor crooners are squeezed between them.

Mencken Counts 'Em

Decibels Hit Ceiling In Keynote-Night Din

PHILADELPHIA, JUNE 21—Just as the Hon. Carroll Reece, chairman of the Republican National Committee, took his stance before the speaker's stand tonight and prepared to wallop the second session of the Republican National Convention to order, there was an uproar behind him, and the whisper went about that the Hon. Arthur H. Vandenberg had appeared on the platform.

Somewhat unusually for whispers in such gatherings, this one turned out to be true. There, indeed, was the veritable Vandenberg, and if not the whole of him then at least his bald head, looming over the mob of Class A lady politicos who rushed up to greet him.

Bounding Michigan Pulses

If the blood of the Taft men and Dewey men ran cold, they gave no sign of it, but the bounding pulses of the Michigan men sent them leaping to the platform, and there they bowled over the sergeants-at-arms and began to paw their hero.

All this made a pretty scene, and such of the spectators as could see it gave a hearty huzzah, but unhappily it was a violation of the convention rules, which forbid mere delegates and alternates to come to the platform without invitations. So the sergeants-at-arms pulled themselves together and proceeded to chase the Michiganders back to their pens on the floor, and in a few minutes the job was accomplished.

A few delegates, resisting this expulsion or at any rate remonstrating against it, were assisted. In brief, they got the bum's rush.

Soprano, Crooner And Choir

At the end of this episode, Vandenberg himself took a seat toward the back of the platform, and the show could go on. There is not much to say about it.

A stout soprano whooped "The Star-Spangled Banner," a

handsome radio crooner with a loud, but not unpleasant voice, roared a few pieces, a small mixed choir tried in vain to outbawl him, and the stage was set for the Hon. Dwight H. Green and his keynote speech.

One of the pieces of the crooner was Schubert's "Ave Maria." It probably got the most vociferous performance ever suffered in recorded history by a composition presumably devotional.

Every Decibel For Schubert

The amplifier system was working beautifully and the boys in the control-room let out every decibel they had. Up, up, up went the crooner from *fff* to *ffff* and then to *ffffff*, *ffffffff*, and *ffffffffffffff*, ending at last, red in the face but delighted, with a tremendous *ffffffffffffffffff*.

Governor Green made a workmanlike job of his keynote speech, but it is hardly to be said that his performance was a knockout. He appeared in the same ensemble that he wore at yesterday's rehearsal, a neat blue suit, a black-and-white checked necktie, and a white shirt and clean collar.

His voice is clear, loud and manly, but there is no variety in it, and after ten minutes it began to sound wooden. He read his speech with such ease that he almost suggested that he had written it himself, but he did not adorn it with any extemporaneous interpolations, or, as Democrats would say, ad-libbing.

Not much applause ruffled his progress. Sometimes five minutes went by without a sound from the delegates and alternates. Most of them sat through it with the dumb, resigned air of cattle waiting in the stockyards.

A few fanned themselves, for the dreadful lights made it hot in the hall. A few others scratched themselves dismally.

Here and there two adjacent ones whispered. What they had to say I did not learn, but apparently it was not exhilarating.

Gate-Giving Promise Pleases

The most earnest clapper-clawing, save at the end, followed the hon. gentleman's solemn promise that the new Republican president, whoever he is, will clean out all the dubious characters who now hog places at the public trough, feasting upon the taxpayers' vitals and disgracing the human race. All these nefarious persons, he said, will get the gate.

Most of the delegates and alternates have been pining and panting for office for fifteen long years, and their pulses race every time they hear that succor is at hand.

Green talked for nearly an hour. The tumult which followed was very feeble and lasted only a few minutes, though it was helped by some heavy blowing by the Petrillo boys in the bandstand, and not at all discouraged by the fact that the speaker himself, now temporary chairman of the convention, remained expectantly at the speaker's stand.

The Luce Forensic Not Pale

Finally, he gave up and introduced the ex-Hon. Clare Boothe Luce, formerly a congresswoman from Connecticut and still one of the salient stateswomen of the Republic.

La Luce had not bothered to take lessons in television makeup, which calls for great gobs of barn or bridge paint, and in consequence the lights made her look very pale. But there was certainly nothing pale about her forensic technique.

Before she had proceeded five minutes she was wrapping the Hon. Mr. Truman in such barbed wires of satire and sarcasm that if he was sitting by the White House radio he must have done a good deal of coughing, and perhaps even a little cussing.

Some of her flights of irony, I suspect, went over the heads of the radio audience whether in or out of White House, as they undoubtedly went over the heads of the delegates and alternates.

Literary And Superior

Nevertheless, the latter seemed to sense that something literary and superior was on tap, and whenever she loosed a phrase that they could fathom at all, they gave her a very polite hand.

When, toward the middle of her discourse, she mentioned the name of Vandenberg, and called him a statesman of high quality, his lieges in the Minnesota delegation leaped up from their hard chairs on the floor and howled frantically, thus hurling their defiance at the sergeants-at-arms who had but lately skidded them from the platform.

When the honorable lady shut down it was after 11 o'clock, and a great many of the spectators began to shuffle out of the hall. At once the Hon. Mr. Green recognized a Tennessee publicist who moved an adjournment, and the convention knocked off until tomorrow morning.

Officially At 10 O'Clock

The orgies of the convention began this morning officially at 10 o'clock but actually at 10:22.

Canto No. 1 was even more banal than usual. When the first

rhetorician up, the Hon. Walter S. Hallanan, chairman of the committee on arrangements, clouted his gavel, the galleries were half empty, and most of the glaring lights were dimmed.

The rest of the morning entertainment sagged below that of an old-time Chautauqua and hardly got above that of a modern radio program. An indifferent soprano in a white-and-blue evening dress sang "The Star-Spangled Banner," and the crowd struggled glooming-ly to its feet.

The Hon. Carroll Reece, chairman of the Republican National Committee, hollered for the American way of life and denounced both the Stalin and Pendergast varieties of democracy. Various lady politicos, one of them reasonably sightly, went to the mike to make routine motions.

Mayor Bernard Samuel, of Philadelphia, bade the delegates and alternates welcome and told them about the early glories of the town but without mentioning its present effort to jug a long file of recreant public officials.

Davis Music Hath Charms

Governor James H. Duff of Pennsylvania, in a Palm Beach suit that matched exactly the muddy blondness of his hair and eyebrows, gave a long speech that nobody appeared to listen to. A barber shop quartette sang.

That was all save for the music of the band, which was excellent. The leader thereof, Prof. Meyer Davis, has assembled 75 really competent musicians, and whenever they break into a Sousa march the horrors of convention oratory are forgotten.

I am glad to give a free reading notice to his trumpeters and especially to his magnificent cymbal player.

Once more as in Beethoven's day, the tone art is the best medicine for the headaches of politics.*

---

*A note in Mencken's scrapbook reads: "I fell ill on June 22, and had to come home, thus missing the rest of the convention.

HLM"

II

The Democrats

Mencken At Gettysburg

Yank Democrats Tense As Rebel Army Nears

PHILADELPHIA, JULY 9—With the advancing Confederate Army still below the Potomac, Philadelphia was steeped tonight in the nervous calm that fell upon it in the days before Gettysburg.

No one knew precisely what was coming, so everybody sought comfort by assuming by that nothing was coming. The only active ganglion in the Democratic nervous system was the Committee on Resolutions, in session since Wednesday on the theory that it is drawing up the party platform.

That theory, of course, is buncombe. The platform, when the time comes, will be sent up from Washington. But, meanwhile, the committee spent the day going through the motions of listening to advocates of a long string of proposed planks.

Cells Of Uplift Galore

These advocates consisted of representatives of almost innumerable cells of the uplift, ranging from the Mothers of America to the National Authority for the Ladies' Handbag Industry, and from the American League for an Undivided Ireland to the United States Committee for a United Nations Genocide Convention.

Today's stars were the Hon. William Green, president of the American Federation of Labor, and the ex-Hon. Leon Henderson, formerly a New Deal wizard and now chairman of Americans for Democratic Action.

Old Bill Green had more time on the stand than any other orator, and under his own steam said the least. His 2,500-word pronunciamento on the issues of the hour was so vague on all crucial issues, and was read in so dull and flabby a manner, that the members of the committee began to needle him before he had got halfway through it; and when he finished at last, they pitched in to clarify it and put teeth in it.

Patriotic Job Of Clarification

This patriotic work was mainly carried on by Senator Scott Lucas, of Illinois, and the chairman, Senator Francis J. Myers, of Pennsylvania, but various other members—including one of the females—also took a hand. The main business of all of them was to induce the witness to say flatly that every one of the current troubles of the country was to be blamed on the Republican majority in Congress, and this they finally induced him to declare.

They had their easiest time while they were on the subject of the hamstringing and denaturizing of the Department of Labor. Lucas allowed that this was the most dreadful example of skullduggery within his recollection, and pointed out indignantly that both the Department of Agriculture and that of Commerce had escaped anything of the sort, thus leaving the industrialists and farmers of the country free to work their wicked will upon the rest of its people.

And Green Agrees They Did

"In other words," said Lucas at the end, "they raped labor. Do you agree to that?" Green replied that he did and the hearing brightened. Lucas then read to him various extracts from the Republican platform, and asked him if he didn't think they showed an implacable enmity to the toiler. He said that he did.

His main points in his prepared statement were that he was strongly in favor of (a) an immediate end to inflation, and (b) a further large increase in wages, especially in the lower brackets.

Comrade Henderson came out eloquently in favor of a foreign policy that "will revitalize the Democratic political forces and the currents of economic activity in Europe and throughout the world," an extension of civil liberties at home, drastic curbs upon the cost of living and the establishment of a continually expanding economy, free of the shackles of monopoly and the threat of "boom and bust."

Proud Of His "Boom and Bust"

He departed from his text long enough to say that he had coined this phrase, "boom and bust" in 1937, and to indicate that he was proud of it. He had with him a long paper proposing forward-looking planks for the party platform, but cheered the committee by refraining from reading it.

The members bore the long ordeal philosophically. While the endless suggestions, declarations and remonstrances of lesser publicists were being read they listened in silence, scratching themselves now and then or gulping beakers of ice water.

The small audience—it never exceeded 100 persons—shuffled and whispered a good deal, and now and then Chairman Myers had to beg it to shut up. The seats reserved for the press were nearly empty, and two of the journalists in attendance leaned back drowsily in their chairs, with their feet propped on other chairs.

Boredom and Hideous Hats

Not a few of the committeemen have been judges in their day, and are thus inured to boredom. Others, for example, General Philip B. Perlman, of Maryland, are studying for the bench, and were apparently glad of the chance to practice. The whole proceedings had the air of a lengthy and interminable suit in equity, with all the chief lawyers taking the afternoon off to play golf, and the arguments pro and con turned over to Class D law clerks.

The loud-speaker system was tuned low, so the noise in the room was inconsiderable, even when lady witnesses were denouncing injustice.

Some of these witnesses wore hats of exaggerated and almost inhuman hideousness. Time was when politics for the fair seemed a pleasant avenue to rich and docile husbands, but in late years the stateswomen appear to have given up hope.

But Roosevelt Looks Grim

The convention hall is being repainted for the Democrats, but in the same baby blue that greeted the Republicans. The only portraits so far hung are one for Roosevelt 2d and one of President Truman. The latter shows His Excellency smiling affably, but Roosevelt looks grim and even somewhat alarmed. Gangs of men are hanging festoons of street-carnival flags and bunting.

The frequent steps on the routes to the platform, which tripped and floored many a Republican three weeks ago, are being replaced with ramps. An elegant green carpet has been laid upon the platform itself.

Mencken Hears The Drums

Anti-Rights Rebs Due, All Armed To The Jaws

PHILADELPHIA, JULY 10—Save for some cavalry patrols and a few spies who arrived by air, the Confederate Army, sworn to knock off President Truman, had not yet got to Philadelphia tonight, and as a result there was an air of confidence among the Yankee hordes already assembled.

A good many of the federal jobholders on the ground, indeed, were sure that the rebels would begin falling to fragments before they crossed the Chickahominy, but it should be added at once that this ease of mind was not shared by those most familiar with the behavior patterns of sub-Potomac politicos.

The species, in fact, is excessively bellicose and even bloodthirsty, and there has not been a Democratic convention in history in which it did not stage a gory bout.

Lovey-Dovey 1936 Convention

Even at the lovey-dovey convention of 1936, with everyone gassed and enchanted by the smell of jobs, some of the southerners, led by the late Cotton Ed Smith, of South Carolina, put on an insurrection against letting colored delegates from the North make speeches.

This time there is more ground for an uproar than at any time for years, for the convention can hardly escape discussing the Hon. Truman's civil-rights program, and if any attempt is made to indorse it as it stands, there will certainly be some loud hollering by the Confederate firebrands, and the more fiery of them may actually take the walk they threaten.

Perlman Reported At Task

The convention bosses, despite their brave talk, are a little anxious about this possibility, and everyone hopes that a way may be found to compromise and reconciliation.

To this end a subcommittee of the resolutions committee has been sweating behind closed doors all day, trying to draw up a plank that will both save civil rights and placate the southerners.

According to the gossip oozing through the locked doors, the lead in this great feat of sophistry is being taken by the Hon. Philip B. Perlman, solicitor general of the United States.

Legal And Journalistic

There are many smart lawyers on the ground, but none other is so well fitted for the task as the Marylander, for he not only knows both canon and civil law inside and out; he also had the advantage, before he tackled Blackstone, of serving on the staff of *The Evening Sun*, and is thus hep to every trick of journalistic double-talk.

How far he has gotten with his dismal job I don't know, for I have been unable to get through his barbed wire today, but it is a fact that he has been getting a great many suggestions through the keyhole, not only from specialists in legal pathology but also from former colleagues in newspaper work.

Cynic's Simple Suggestion

One of the latter, a cynic on the staff of the St. Louis *Post-Dispatch*, sent in a proposed plank this afternoon reading as follows:

"We are for all of President Truman's civil-rights recommendations—and for white supremacy."

Chairman Francis J. Myers, of the resolutions committee (he is not a member of the subcommittee of sophists), submitted to a long press conference today without letting even the smallest kitten out of the bag. He declared, no doubt truthfully, that he had no idea how the plank would read when completed, but seemed to incline toward the theory that it would resemble the 1944 plank, which said nothing.

Rose Water Or Gasoline

That plank was drawn up, however, before Dr. Truman cut loose with his revolutionary program, and hence before the Confederates took to the war path. What was a spray of rose water in 1944 may turn out to be a squirt of gasoline next week.

The agendum of the convention postpones the report of the resolutions committee until Wednesday, but there will undoubtedly be demands that it be brought in on Tuesday, or maybe even Monday.

Myers reported that extraordinary precautions will be taken to keep it secret until it is presented on the floor, but that plan may be very easily upset by the advance of journalistic science.

Three weeks ago the Republicans had the same idea, but a woman reporter sneaked into their Kremlin and had the whole platform in type for her paper before their resolutions committee tumbled to what was happening.

Douglas Still Boomed

Though Supreme Court Justice William O. Douglas has declared categorically that he doesn't itch to grab the nomination from Truman, he has not said that he wouldn't take it if it were thrust upon him, so his propagandists keep up a noisy clatter.

They are chiefly very young men, and seem to be innocently unaware that nominations are made by the votes of delegates, not by the distribution of buttons. They have some delegates, to be sure, but not enough to make any impression upon the great swarm of Truman jobholders, and it is hard to imagine the Confederates coming over to their man.

Baby Spotlight On Tydings

Myers was asked today if he was for Douglas for second place on the ticket, but got rid of the question with a delicate flow of words. He was then asked if the White House inclined that way, but replied that he had not discussed the matter with the White House.

The report about town is that Truman, as a middle westerner, favors a running mate from either the West Coast or the East Coast.

This turns a baby spotlight on Senator Tydings, of Maryland, who is the official choice of the state delegation, but most of the members of the delegation seem to be actually for Governor Lane, who can't be an open candidate.

Eisenhower Sergeant Unstilled

The Eisenhower boom is dying in dreadful agony. The general himself has taken a Sherman runout powder, but his more rampant followers, led by his old mess sergeant, Marty Snyder, are still going about the Philadelphia streets in a jeep fitted with a loud-speaker, whooping and howling for him.

Comrade Snyder told me today that he would stick until the last galoot was ashore—that is, until the convention had made a nomination, whether of his hero or another.

He hands out the words of an Eisenhower song written by Mayhew Lake, a student of the late George M. Cohan, and when the phonograph hitched to the loud-speaker sounds the music a good many idlers join Marty and his *aide-de-camp*, John Schwartz, in the singing.

Campaign-Song Prospects

The words have only the palest sort of literary merit, but the music is not bad, and if the general could be kidnapped and nominated the combination would make a good campaign song—at all events, one better than Truman's poets and composers are likely to fetch up.

With the Eisenhower campaign headquarters reduced to a jeep, the only one that remains open is that of the Douglas boys. No one ever drops in to hear their message, so they go on the street and flag passers-by.

They pin a button on every one who doesn't wave them off, and distribute pamphlets and handbills describing the learned justice as a forward-looker beyond compare, with a heart that busts whenever he thinks of the underprivileged.

Flag Of The Free State

I doubt that they will discover any concern for the underprivileged in the approaching legions of Lee, Longstreet, Stonewall Jackson and Jeb Stuart.

The heelers in charge of the arrangement of the hall added the flags of all the states to the bunting left over from the Republican convention.

The flag of the Free State, though it has a bad spot on the gallery rail, shines out among the ill-designed and banal ensigns of the other states like a wart on a bald head. Saving the flags of Texas and Alaska, it is the only one that may be plausibly described as beautiful.

Press Reshuffled By Parties

The same heelers have done some reshuffling in the press-stand. Such Republican papers as the Chicago *Tribune*, the New York *Herald-Tribune* and the Boston *Herald* have been demoted to places further from the speakers' platform than they had three weeks ago, and the principal Democratic papers have been moved up.

I record without comment the news that the pew of the *Sunpapers* is now two rows forward of what it was before.

This morning some wag pasted a huge photograph of Eisenhower upon the front of the speakers' stand. It will be torn off, I daresay, before the orgies begin.

Mencken Is Let Down

Trumanocide Rebels' Verbal Guns Go Phut

PHILADELPHIA, JULY 11—The Confederates who poured into Philadelphia this morning to put the kibosh on President Truman were considerably subdued by the evening.

They held their caucus in the afternoon, and had their say on his high crimes and misdemeanors, but there was very little bite or zowie in their execrations, and they broke up at least pretty well convinced, and even admitting openly, that there was really nothing much that they could do about it.

Toward the end of their pow-wow in the Benjamin Franklin Hotel, their chairman, Governor Ben T. Laney, of Arkansas, ordered them to stand up by delegations, and their strength was thus revealed to the Truman spies who swarmed in the hall.

One Copperhead Applauded

This reckless self-exposure showed that while Alabama, Florida, Mississippi and one or two other states were fairly well represented, there were only twelve present from Virginia, only two each from Georgia and Louisiana, and only one from Oklahoma.

After the count of bayonets the Hon. Mr. Laney asked if there were any copperheads present from *partibus infidelium*. A lone Trumanocide from Indiana then made himself known, and was politely applauded. But there were no others, and the gathering broke up in depressed spirits. It will meet again tomorrow, but without much hope.

The difficulty lies in the fact that it has no candidate to pit against the civil-rights heretic.

Doubts About Barkley

There are, of course, plenty who stand in waiting, but all are poisonous. Even the Hon. Alben Barkley, of Kentucky, who was formally put in nomination, is a weak sister, for many believe that Truman could fetch him by offering him the vice-presidency, or even a federal judgeship.

Senator Pepper, of Florida, is willing to the point of enthusiasm, but there is no visible libido for him.

Some of the speakers, in fact, admitted frankly that Truman could not be beaten; for it is an old maxim in politics that something cannot be beaten by nothing.

To Strike Blow For Principle

But all agreed that the main business ahead is not actually to slaughter him, but to strike a blow, powerful if vain, for the imperishable principle of States' Rights.

This will be done, it was announced, on the floor of the convention. The resolutions committee appointed today will report a platform in opposition to the official or White House platform, and an earnest fight for it will be made.

Unluckily, the rebels neglected to bring with them a squad of rhetoricians fit for the job. The only speaker who showed any form today was Governor J. Strom Thurmond, of South Carolina, and he spoke a great deal more like a soldier than a rabble-rouser.

Instruction of Electors

His argument, in brief, was that it will not be necessary to vote for Dewey in November. A simpler, more effective and less revolting plan will be to choose presidential electors sworn to cast their ballots for some high-toned southerner, but who this southerner should be Governor Thurmond did not say.

While he was speaking the Hon. Jimmie Roosevelt, now of California, sneaked into the hall accompanied by Senator Olin D. Johnston, like Thurmond, of South Carolina, and a suite of admirers. He was preceded by a mob of photographers exploding flashlights, and for a few moments there was a great craning of necks. But Jimmie was not introduced, and presently retired without announcing the purpose of his visit.

Thurmond concluded his remarks by predicting that Truman will not get a single electoral vote from the South.

Country Editor Pleases

The other speakers were all bush leaguers. The only one who got any appreciable applause was the Hon. Jimmie Arrington, a country editor from Collins, Mississippi, a whistle stop deep in the Bible country.

He had nothing to say, but he said it in a rustic way that pleased both the delegates and the gallery. To almost every affirmative sentence he added "He certainly did," "She certainly was," "They certainly don't" or the like, and after twenty or thirty repetitions a flutter of snickers greeted every recurrence.

He also related some instructive anecdotes from Mississippi folklore. But otherwise he fell as flat as the others.

Totalitarian Unanimity

Chairman Laney also got the tribute of chuckles for his way of putting questions. "All those in favor," he would roar, "will say aye." Then he would add, "All those opposed will say aye."

By the use of this totalitarian system he got unanimous approval for all the resolutions adopted. What they were about was obscure in most cases, and in many it was wholly unintelligible. But everyone knew that the fundamental content of each and every one was hostility to Dr. Truman.

A gentleman named Meyers, hailing from Kentucky but claiming to have a wife from Mississippi, made a somewhat painful impression by referring to the Confederates as rebels.

Faux Pas In South

This is almost as much a *faux pas* in the actual South as using you-all in the singular, and it was predicted by many that he would hear from his Mississippi lady on the subject when he got home.

He hollered for Alben Barkley, but for the reasons already stated he got no second. No other candidate was proposed by name.

The revolutionists came rolling in from the South all morning on trains that were from ten minutes to two hours late. The Floridians had the platforms of their Pullmans piled high with cases of Miami beer, but there was no sign of the oranges, grapefruit, lemons, limes, tangerines, cumquats, and other fruits that people from their state used to bring to Democratic national conventions.

Notable For Becoming Hats

It was remarked at the caucus that very few of the delegates and alternates looked like southerners, as southerners are commonly visualized by northerners. They actually looked a good deal more like

Rotarians from the Middle West, and only a few of those heard in the caucus showed southern speech-ways.

The Alabamians are reported to have traveled all the way from Birmingham without getting down a single carboy of white mule, or loosing a single rebel yell.

The females accompanying all the delegations seemed to be the antitheses of the standard lady politician, for many of them wore becoming hats and weighed less than 160 pounds, and not a few of the younger ones were very toothsome.

On Altar Of Service

What will come of Senator Pepper's immolation on the altar of service remains to be seen. He is admired in most parts of the South with a frenzy only a degree or two less virulent than the frenzy for Truman.

He claims to have several hundred votes sewed up, but so did the late Harold Stassen, the Minnesota toy balloon.

The man the Confederates really need is Gerald L.K. Smith. But Gerald has been so long derided and defamed by Communists, Darwinians, New Dealers, agnostics, atheists, antinomians and other such miscreants that his fame is somewhat tarnished, and it would probably be a bad idea to send for him. Moreover, it is generally believed that he is a Republican.

Mencken Wipes Brow

'Dear Alben,' All Het Up Over GOP, Mops His, Too

PHILADELPHIA, JULY 12—The Hon. Alben W. Barkley's keynote speech to the Democratic National Convention tonight ran close to the pattern of tradition. That is to say, it was long, loud and feverish, but threw very little light upon the issues of the hour.

On the critical question of civil rights it got no further than ratifying those specified by the Declaration of Independence. The southern rebels against the Truman program seemed almost willing yesterday to accept the hon. gentleman as their rump candidate for the presidency. There was no reason before the house tonight that they should reject him as Truman's running mate.

Cut To Hour And Seven Minutes

His speech ran 1 hour and 7 minutes. The original text, as it was prepared with the aid of the party literati, would have taken at least two hours. But the night was hot, and the speaker slashed it mercilessly as he went along. Sometimes he omitted a whole paragraph, and there were very few that did not suffer some trimming.

Not infrequently he departed from his script altogether and soared into the empyrean of the extempore. In these flights he was at his best, for he is a rabble-rouser of great gifts, and knows precisely how to tickle a crowd.

But the job before him was not easy, even for a virtuoso, for the heat of the evening made it difficult for either speaker or audience to concentrate upon the official statistics which formed the core of his discourse.

Figures Not Easy Listening

Some of these statistics proved that the New Deal has saved the American people from a tremendous series of disasters, and the rest proved that the Republicans, when they were in power, had done more actual damage than both world wars.

Unfortunately, figures are not easy listening, and the audience did not rise to them with any enthusiasm.

"Dear Alben" appeared to find them difficult himself, and sometimes paused in his roaring to find his place among them. He got the most huzzahs when he indulged himself in country humor.

Undernourished Spiders

Once he said that when the Hoover administration came to its gloomy end the very spiders of Washington were so weak from undernourishment that they could barely weave the cobwebs needed to drape the stricken government offices.

The crowd guffawed loudly at that one.

Another time he defined a bureaucrat as a Democrat who holds some office that a Republican wants. This also set them to whooping.

Despite such interludes of relief, the delegates and alternates appeared to suffer severely during his speech. Penned in their hard narrow seats, they were gradually reduced to something resembling a colloidal state. The hon. gentleman himself made equally heavy weather of it.

27 Minutes of Demonstration

Perspiration ran down his nose and dripped from his chin, and his elegant Palm Beach suit looked more and more like a wet towel. But he hung on manfully, and when he finished at last he was still ready for a few more howls.

His speech was followed by a demonstration designed to promote his vice-presidential chances, but though it lasted 27 minutes, it was pretty feeble, and even at its loudest seemed more pumped up than spontaneous.

Only one placard was in line, and that was provided by the candidate's fellow-Kentuckians. A good many of the standards of other states appeared in the procession, and before the rostrum, but the parade never got very wild.

Tydings Presented To Audience

When it was over, various dignitaries were summoned to the platform and presented to the audience.

Among them were Senator Tydings, who had earlier in the evening pulled out of the vice-presidential race in favor of Barkley, and

Governor Lane, who had refused to let the Maryland delegation substitute him for Tydings. Others who were shown were Senator O'Conor, Jimmie Roosevelt and a dozen or more Class B senators.

During these exercises the delegates and alternates began to escape to the downtown soda fountains, and most of the people in the galleries staggered out too. But there were two lady orators waiting to be heard, and there was no holding them.

Cost-Of-Living Lecture

The first was the Hon. India Edwards, executive director of the women's division of the Democratic National Committee. Clad in a severely black gown and a round, white hat, she delivered a solemn lecture in a hard, brittle voice.

There was some confusion in the emptying hall, and so it was hard to get the drift of her remarks, but apparently her subject was a cost of living, for at one point she fetched a naked beefsteak out of a paper bag and held it up to view, and at another time she lifted a little girl to the speaker's stand and pointed lugubriously to the child's shoes and frock.

She also exhibited a bottle of milk and inflated a toy balloon, but it was impossible to make out what these horrors signified.

Ma Perkins Defends Politics

By the time she subsided it was a quarter to twelve, but the next (and last) lady orator was undaunted by either the lateness of the hour or the sufferings of the surviving Democrats.

She was the celebrated Ma Perkins, one of the great glories of the Roosevelt administrations.

Her speech was a vigorous defense of politics and politicians, though she did not go so far as to mention names. "Politics," she said, "fulfills man's essential and permanent function as a social being, as a part of God's creation."

The politicos still present seemed to be pleased to hear that they were a part of God's creation, but their applause got no further than a few handclaps, for la Perkins banged away without giving them a chance to yell.

F.D.R. Allusion Divined

She ended with a word picture of a great statesman of the recent past—a man who lifted political endeavor to heights that it had never previously attained, and would be remembered for 10,000 or 20,000 years by a grateful and marveling posterity.

Again she refrained from mentioning names, but some of the brighter delegates and alternates divined that she had reference to the late FDR. Several times during her discourse she backed off the mike, and as a result her voice toned down to a hoarse whisper.

Barkley tiptoed up and steered her back, and the hullabaloo that issues normally from the loud-speaker was resumed.

Too Young For Yesteryear

The evening session, scheduled to begin at 8:30, was not actually clouted to order until 9:07, but there was a preliminary half hour of song, led by both organ and band.

The band had brought with it a quartet of crooners, and they sought to heat up the incoming crowd with the ballads of yesteryear, but it quickly turned out to be impossible.

The reason was plain enough: At least two thirds of the spectators were too young to remember them. They were unborn when "Little Annie Rooney" was in its prime, and even "The Sidewalks of New York" caught them in school. It was too hot in the hall for a songfest.

Prayer And Anthem

There ensued a prayer by a bishop and singing of "The Star-Spangled Banner" by an Irish tenor. Both brought the crowd to its feet. Meanwhile, the news photographers roved the hall snapping celebrities, including a colored lady delegate from Indiana.

The Kentucky delegation, sniffing the trend to Barkley, staged a tableau showing a large sign prepared for the anticipated demonstration. Two delegates, male and female, held it aloft and gyrated before it in attitudes of enthusiasm.

At 9:35 "Dear Alben" himself was introduced by Chairman McGrath, and began his long keynote speech. He got a hearty hand as he appeared, but it was some time before his remarks evoked any save the most formal applause.

Mencken Lifts An Eyebrow

The Pretty Lady-Democrats Brighten Up A Dull Scene

PHILADELPHIA, JULY 12—The convention heaved itself into being and sentience this afternoon at 12:05, 35 minutes late.

The opening exercises were of the usual boresome imbecility. Bad speakers, one after another, did their stuff while the delegates and alternates milled in the aisles and the sparse mob in the galleries steadily melted away.

Mayor David Lawrence, of Pittsburgh, who was sent in to call the meeting to order and introduce Cardinal Dougherty, of Philadelphia, the official chaplain of the afternoon, launched into a long harangue, while His Eminence waited with archiepiscopal fortitude for the mike.

Parade of Rhetoricians

Among the disturbers of the peace were Senator J. Howard McGrath, of Rhode Island, chairman of the Democratic National Committee; Senator Francis J. Myers, of Pennsylvania; the Hon. Bernard Samuel, of Philadelphia (a Republican, and hence booed by the Democratic gallery); the Hon. Arthur C. Kaufmann, president of the Philadelphia Chamber of Commerce, and an eminent realtor named Albert Greenfield, who raised the money to bring the convention to town.

In this dismal parade of rhetoricians there were two exhilarating breaks. First: Miss Lucy Munroe was put up to lead the congregation in moaning and gargling "The Star-Spangled Banner." She turned out to have a good voice, and made a creditable job of it.

More, she was fair to look upon and had on a frock so well made that it must have set her back a pretty penny.

Everyone glowed with delight, and the newsreel boys and newspaper photographers fought viciously to get up close.

But the real surprise came when Mrs. Dorothy M. Vredenburgh, of Alabama, secretary of the Democratic National Committee, arose belatedly to read the call for the convention. Lady politicians not infrequently resemble British tramp steamers dressed for the King's birthday, but this one, like la Munroe, was slim, pretty and smartly clad, so the various delegations gave her hearty huzzahs as she came to their states.

Memorials On Schedule

Even her revelation that North Dakota would have eight votes got a flutter of applause.

Tomorrow evening the convention will pause in its lucubrations long enough to stage a lodge of sorrow in memory of the late President Roosevelt, with the heroes of World War II thrown in. A battery of army and navy chaplains has been engaged to give the affair liturgical splendor and there will be a eulogy of FDR by a California orator.

The next morning there will be a second memorial service in a downtown eating house, with William Jennings Bryan, Woodrow Wilson and Josephus Daniels added to the list of immortals honored.

Mencken Gets His Battle

Rebs Breach Doghouse, Defiant Guns A-Barkin'

PHILADELPHIA, JULY 13—The Confederates, after two days in the doghouse, broke out on the floor of the Democratic National Convention tonight, and in an instant the hall was wild with yells, howls, bellows, whoops and execrations.

No one knew as yet what the dilatory Committee on Resolutions was going to have to say about the Truman civil-rights program, but a chance came to sound off on the subject when the Committee on Credentials brought in its report.

Report Seems Innocent

That report, innocent enough on its face, seated the delegation from Mississippi despite its solemn vow to walk out unless the candidates for both president and vice-president repudiated the program and promised to sin no more.

At once a colored delegate named George L. Vaughan, hailing from St. Louis, leaped to the mike with a violent protest. He had gone for less than a minute when there were howls of "No, No" from Florida, and the state standard began to sway and wobble as if it had suddenly become alive.

It was a banal enough signal, but it was enough to set off a turmoil that roared from end to end of the hall.

Negro Not Perturbed

Comrade Vaughan, a large and very dark Negro with a smooth glistening head, was not perturbed. On the contrary, he faced the uproar boldly, and defied it in a loud, brassy voice. What he had to say, precisely, was not always clear in the press-stand, for the noise quickly became ear splitting, but whatever it was he kept on shouting it with magnificent calm.

When he shut down at last it appeared that he had offered a

minority report from the Committee on Credentials, denouncing the Confederates as enemies of democracy and jumping the gun on the Committee on Resolutions by coming out flatly for the whole Truman program.

Only Senator Carl Hatch, of New Mexico, argued formally for the majority report, and he spoke no more than a minute, but when the two reports were put to a vote the majority won by a substantial excess of yells.

Defeat Without Grief

The Confederates took their defeat without repining. When the result was announced, various pro-Truman states demanded to have it recorded that they had voted for the minority report.

Barkley said that the rules did not provide for this but that he would permit it as a courtesy.

The first to go on record was Illinois and the second was New York. California, clamoring for a chance to follow, made such an uproar that its spokesman, John F. Shelly, was permitted to come to the platform to say its say. The following other states later made known that they were of like mind: Connecticut, Iowa, Michigan, Minnesota, Nevada, Ohio, Pennsylvania, Washington, Wisconsin and the District of Columbia. Altogether they cast a good deal fewer votes than were needed to upset the majority report.

Itching For Roughhouse

By this time the convention was beginning to show old-time Democratic form. That is to say, it was itching for roughhouse. Another chance came when Senator Herbert O'Conor, of Maryland, brought in the report of the Committee on Rules.

This report said nothing about the two-thirds rule, abrogated in 1932, but the southerners at once moved to restore it, and for twenty minutes their orator hollered for it loudly.

The only delegate to argue against it was the Hon. Oscar Ewing, a Class A Truman jobholder, but it was lost by a large majority, and so another Confederate scheme to knock out Truman came to nothing.

The two battles, though brisk and noisy, did not shed more than a lake or two of blood, and the defeated army retired in good order to a prepared position in the swamps bordering the Suwanee River. What it will do tomorrow is unknown at this writing.

The hall is full of rumors tonight that the Hon. Philip B. Perlman and his fellow sophists have at least concocted a platform that will both satisfy Harlem and preserve segregation in Alabama, but its text is still kept secret.

The rest of the evening's proceedings were dull and dismal. The Hon. Sam Rayburn, of Texas, on his election as permanent chairman, made a speech that set him to sweating alarmingly, but no one appeared to pay any attention to it.

He was followed by the Hon. Mary T. Norton, of New Jersey, who delivered a long discourse that was mainly unintelligible here. She is a lady of settled years, wearing sober black and horn-rimmed glasses, and she looks a great deal like the better sort of bourgeois Baltimore housewife.

Lodge Of Sorrow Opens

The lodge of sorrow began at 8:50 with the entrance of color guards representing all branches of the armed forces. As soon as the flags were planted in the space before the speakers' stand, Lawrence Tibbett, the opera singer, was sent to the mike to sing "The Star-Spangled Banner."

He made a dreadful mess of it. Starting too high for his baritone voice, he was presently forced to drop an octave to avoid strangling. Then he made a second attempt on the high ones, and was baffled again. He retired in considerable discomfiture. The delegates and alternates applauded him politely but not vociferously.

Fifteen minutes later, after a colored choir had sung Martin Luther's famous hymn, "A Mighty Fortress Is Our God," Tibbett was given a second crack at the mike, and sang a setting of the Lord's Prayer. This time he fetched each and every note and the crowd gave him a cheer.

The memorial service lasted until 9:45. Chairman Barkley turned it over to Mayor William O'Dwyer, of New York, who ran it in a neat and dignified manner. The speakers were only four in number.

The first was Bishop William R. Arnold, formerly chief of chaplains of the Army; the second was Van Heflin, a patriotic movie actor; the third was Dr. Aryeh Lev, a Jewish rabbi, and the fourth was Captain Francis Lee Albert, a Protestant chaplain in the Navy.

All of these gentlemen were brief. Captain Albert, in fact, made no speech at all, but instead offered an extemporaneous prayer. Before he began he cautioned the delegates and alternates to bow their heads and close their eyes. Some did so, but not many.

The afternoon session was so dull that most of the delegates and alternates, after sampling a canto or two of it, sneaked back to the downtown saloons. For the first time in recent convention history the newsreel boys did not expose an inch of film.

Even when, after two solid hours of speeches, a passel of cuties came to the platform, and "Dear Alben," after some coy hesitation, began to buss them, the newsreelers sneered at the show as too corny for their public.

The orators were Roy Baker, president of the Young Democratic Clubs of America; Oscar R. Ewing, administrator of the Federal Security Agency; Michael J. Kirwan, chairman of the Democratic Congressional Committee, and Mrs. Charles M. Tillett, vice chairman of the Democratic National Committee.

Loud Accent On Idealism

Baker, a loud young man, bellered for idealism for half an hour, winding up with a quotation from the late FDR urging all politicians to be dreamers. There were no apparent takers, and even the magic name evoked only a sputter of applause. Ewing howled for more and more money for his clients, and denounced the Republicans in Congress for withholding it.

Kirwan drew a gruesome picture of life in Hooverian days, and Mrs. Tillett argued that the only way to attain world peace is to re-elect Truman. She read her speech from a manuscript written in so large a hand that there were but fifteen or twenty words to a page.

Mrs. Tillett is a slim and good-looking woman, and had on a charming frock and a becoming hat, so she presented an agreeable contrast to the common run of lady politicos, most of whom eat too much and have no taste in dress. Profiting by the dreadful experience of the Hon. Clare Boothe Luce at the Republican convention, she had an able technician make her up for the television lights, and he did a good job with his barn paints.

Seen But Not Heard

But by the time she went on no one in the hall could endure another speech, so the survivors contented themselves with admiring her without listening to her.

Miss Carol Brice, a colored contralto with a powerful voice and a brisk and business-like air, did "The Star-Spangled Banner" at the start of the orgies and later returned with a couple of spirituals.

Who the cuties were who fetched old Alben I did not learn. He crowned one of them with a wreath of flowers. The crowd urged him to kiss them, but he hung back for quite a while.

Doves For The Victors

Truman And Barkley Emerge Amid Uproar

PHILADELPHIA, THURSDAY, JULY 15*—It was half past one this morning before President Truman got to the platform of the Democratic National Convention to accept his nomination, though he had been stored away in another part of the hall, surrounded by his family, his friends and a large force of Secret Service men, for hours.

He was escorted in by six former chairmen of the Democratic National Committee and accompanied by Mrs. Truman and their daughter, Margaret. With them came the vice-presidential nominee, Senator and Mrs. Barkley, and their daughter, Mrs. Max O. Truitt.

The Ladies Look Bewildered

The ladies were simply dressed—Mrs. Barkley and Mrs. Truitt in black, and Miss Margaret in a white sweater and a blue figured skirt. All three looked bewildered and made off as soon as possible.

Chairman Rayburn had asked the crowd to attempt no prolonged demonstration when the candidates marched in, but there was naturally a great uproar, and the band fomented it by playing "Hail to the Chief" and "My Old Kentucky Home."

Rayburn tried to shut off this music, but for some time he did not succeed. This irritated him, and he banged his gavel violently. The band, however, continued to blow to the bitter end. And when it finished Mrs. Emma Guffey Miller, sister to the celebrated Joe Guffey

---

*Mencken wrote three leads on the session that began the afternoon of July 14 and carried over into the early hours of July 15, all under a July 15 dateline. The first was that the "embattled Confederates got a double mauling," on the civil-rights plank of the platform, and on their failure to block Truman. The second was that Truman was nominated "to the tune of immense cataracts and bad oratory," then "held in storage" by the secret service until time to make his acceptance speech. The final version, printed here, incorporated most of the earlier stories, save for transitional paragraphs which Mencken deleted in the rewriting.

and a power in Pennsylvania politics, rushed to the mike to present the two candidates with a replica of the Liberty Bell.

Doves Cooped In Liberty Bell

There was a door in it, and when the door was open half a dozen white doves flew out. They at once began to dart about the hall, and it was five or six minutes before they were shooed out. Rayburn himself caught one, but let it go again.

Barkley accepted first. He wore a blue coat, light striped pants, a white shirt and collar and a somewhat florid blue tie. It took him only a few minutes to immolate himself on the altar of patriotism.

Truman, in a white Palm Beach suit and wearing a gaudy convention badge, followed immediately. The burden of his remarks is reported by able and reliable colleagues. He looked very cocky, and talked accordingly.

"Dear Alben's" Rivals Fade

Every time he made a point, the delegates and alternates loosed huzzahs. The gallery duly joined in, but by this time the gallery had thinned out and far fewer persons heard the president than saw him nominated.

"Dear Alben" fared even better. All of his rivals quickly faded out, and he was put through by acclamation. He had disappeared from the hall long before this and sat with the presidential party in productive custody.

Truman's speech, as I have hinted, was full of fire. It was devoted mainly to excoriating the Republican Congress, and he gave plenty of indication that it is to be his whipping boy in his campaign.

The first real whoops came when he announced that he was calling it back in special session on July 26, and that he would keep it at work until it cured all the evils that currently afflict the country.

They Clasp Hands And Pose

This he said, would not take more than fifteen days—that is, provided the Republicans buckled down to the business, and paid heed to their own platform.

His speech ran about 25 minutes. At its conclusion he and Barkley clasped hands and posed for the newsreel and television boys. But this lasted for only a few minutes, and then they were gone. Sam Rayburn later brought the ladies of their party to the front of the stand, and there was more photographing and the band played loudly. Truman and Barkley presently rejoined them, but only briefly.

And At 2:30, Adjournment

At 2:25 the irascible Rayburn bawled out the photographers, and gavelled for order. At 2:30 he announced that the convention was adjourned.

Thirteen Alabamians took their threatened walk last night in protest against the civil-rights plank, and Mississippi followed them, but when the roll was called, the remainder of Alabama's delegation cast its 26 votes for Russell, though Mississippi remained *non est*.

The border states, Maryland, Kentucky and West Virginia, went for Truman, but the rest of the South joined Alabama in voting for Russell, to wit: Arkansas, Florida, Georgia, Louisiana, the two Carolinas, Tennessee, Texas and Virginia.

But They Couldn't Stop Truman

This solidarity, however, did not muster enough votes to stop Truman. This would have been true even if the two-thirds rule had been revived, which it was not.

The last session of the convention went on in great heat, and was marked by torrents of ninth-rate oratory. On the call of states dozens of speeches were made, and when some of the delegations divided, and had to be polled, many of the individual delegates attempted to speak too. They were slapped down by the chairman, but not until fifteen or twenty of them had got in some useful gurgling for the radio back home.

The walkout of the Alabamians was carried out quietly. Their state, as everyone knows, leads the alphabetical roll of states. When it was called, the Hon. Handy Ellis arose from his place in the delegation and demanded to be heard on a question of personal privilege.

Rayburn invited him to state it, and he read a brief statement into the delegation's mike on the floor. Its delegation, he said, had been elected with instructions to withdraw from the convention in the event that President Truman were nominated or a platform were adopted embodying the hated civil-rights plank.

The latter catastrophe, he continued, was now history and the former was impending. Accordingly, Alabama was taking to the bush, and part of Mississippi would join it.

The Alabamians then rose from their places and stalked toward the door, carrying their state flag and their convention standard with them. So far there had been strangely little excitement in the hall. But now the whole mob rose to its legs and began to howl.

Some Boos, But Mostly Cheers

There were boos in the turmoil, but mostly, it seemed to me, there were cheers. The crowd was against the retreating Confederates, but on the whole it seemed to be friendly, and there was not the slightest sign of hostility.

Just as the state standard got to the rear door it was seized by a woman delegate from Alabama, Mrs. Lucille Patterson, and brought back to the state's place on the floor.

There then issued from the delegation's mike the voice of Senator Lister Hill, a statesman torn between his enthusiasm for the New Deal and his Hippocratic oath to Alabama.

Confused Demonstration

What he had to say was simply that Alabama yielded its place on the roll. Georgia, it appeared, had chosen the Hon. Charles J. Bloch, of Macon, as its spokesman, and he was presently at the platform mike putting in nomination the name of Senator Richard B. Russell, a New Deal fanatic on everything save race relations.

Bloch made a longish speech, and while he was working it off, the noise in the hall steadily increased. The moment he shut down, a dozen state standards began to move in the aisles, and a somewhat confused demonstration was in progress.

Basically, it must have been for Russell, but actually there were dozens of Truman banners in it. The band, so far, had been silent, but Rayburn now gave it the signal to cut loose, and it burst into "Dixie."

This, of course, lifted the amperage of the uproar, but it did not halt the countermovement for Truman, and soon Rayburn had to go to the mike and plead that the Russellites be permitted to do their stuff unmolested. But by this time they were pretty well used up, and in a few moments the noise suddenly ceased.

Rayburn held off his signal to the band for at least ten minutes. Apparently he did not want to have it thought that he was itching, as a southerner, to help the Russell demonstration.

Conspiracy Fails

The silence seemed curious and reports reached the press-stand that Truman agitators had gone to the bandstand and were trying to induce the leader to play "Marching Through Georgia." If this was true, it was a conspiracy that failed. Once "Dixie" was begun the band played it steadily until the musicians ran out of wind.

When Arizona, the second state on the roll, yielded to Missouri, Governor Phil M. Donnelly, of that great state, was sent up to put Truman in nomination.

Such speeches are always third-rate, but this one was worse than most. Moreover, it was delivered very badly. Donnelly, who had a harsh, metallic voice, is tall, and his remarks were discharged above the mike, and hence were barely heard.

A platform functionary lifted the mike after a few minutes and after that the speaker got on better, but he never got on really well. In some lights he looked exactly like Truman. There must be standardized Missourians.

Vociferous As Usual

He launched the magic name at 9:20 and at once the band, by now recovered from "Dixie," blasted into the "Missouri Waltz," aided by the convention organ and another band on the floor.

The ensuing demonstration was as vociferous as usual, but it showed very little imagination. For the most part, it consisted of a dogged plodding through the aisles.

Some of the participants bawled and screamed, but most were silent. Some carried placards, but most simply hoofed along, sweating dismally. The toy horns, party hats and other such tools of merry-making on view were all of 10-cent store quality.

The legends on the banners that waved by all were trite and some were close to idiotic. A few specimens: "The World Hope—Truman," "Illinois Housewives for Truman," "Harvard Students Club for Truman," "The Friend of the Common Man," "Don't Wish: Work for Truman," "Finish the Story With Truman," "New York: Everyone for Truman," "Stop Stalin: Back Truman," "Truman, Foe of Privilege," "Great in '48 With Truman," and "Missouri for Truman."

"Peace For All Time"

But the principal banner, outnumbering all others taken together, was a simple portrait of Harry on a card perhaps 2 feet by 3½, with the following quotation from one of his recent state papers: "Our goal must be, not peace in our time, but peace for all time."

Unless Maryland and West Virginia be counted southern, no southern state took part in the demonstration. The standards of

Alabama and Mississippi had departed for parts unknown before it began, and those of Georgia, Louisiana, Tennessee and the Carolinas stood immovable from end to end. But Hawaii, Puerto Rico and the Virgin Islands all paraded.

After the uproar had gone on for half an hour or so, a basket surmounted by a bell of artificial flowers was hoisted down the platform to the speakers' stand, and from the bell leaped an Indian in füll war-dress.

The Indian thereupon did some monkey-shines for the newsreels and television, but what they signified, if anything, I do not know. In all the show there was not a trace of wit or humor, and save for the lobster and potato of Maine, not a sign of aptness.

It might have been staged just as appropriately for Tom Dewey or the Swami Wallace. I should note an exception from the Michigan corral. It consisted of one of the Truman portrait cards with the hon. gentleman's lips elegantly lipsticked and large patches of rouge on his two cheeks.

At 10 o'clock Rayburn began rapping for order. The crowd obeyed instantly, obviously worn out by the mummery. But the band, for some reason, kept on playing, and it took a lot more banging of the gavel to shut it off.

The hall, by this time, was almost unbearably hot, and as the chairman plied his weapon, sweat ran down his cheeks and off his chin, and he had to pause every few seconds to mop his bald head.

When the call of the roll was resumed Arkansas passed, but California, which followed, sent up Will Rogers, Jr., to second the nomination of Truman. Young Rogers, son of the late comedian, is a Hollywood friend of humanity and once served in Congress as a New Dealer. He was blown up in the explosion of 1946, but has hopes of coming back.

Gavel Goes To McCormack

After Rogers retired, Rayburn himself retired, at least temporarily. Saying that he was somewhat used up, he handed the gavel to the Hon. John W. McCormack, of Massachusetts, his predecessor as Democratic leader in the House.

What actually took him off was the fact that Truman had got to town from Washington, and was waiting in an ante-chamber.

Meanwhile, the rattle of seconding speeches went on. Mrs. Marguerite Peyton Thompson, of Slida, Colorado, did the job prettily for that great state, and following her came the Hon. Thomas J. Dodd, of Connecticut, who began by saying that he would speak only one minute, got a loud cheer for it, and then made good.

Delaware then yielded to the state of Washington, which sent up its governor, Mon C. Wallgren, a handsome fellow and Truman's chief buddy, but nevertheless a bore in a hot hall at 10:30 P.M.

McNutt's Name Presented

When Florida's turn came a local Hampden, the Hon. Byrd Sims, nominated the Hon. Paul McNutt, of Indiana, from the floor. No one laughed.

Georgia yielded to Alabama, and one Carmichael seconded Russell. Idaho yielded to Pennsylvania, which sent one Kane to second Truman.

Illinois sent up one Adamowski for the same purpose. Indiana, passing over McNutt, fell in line likewise as did Iowa and Kansas. Kentucky stood mute.

Louisiana reported that up to this morning it had intended to nominate its governor, Earl Long, a brother to the late Kingfish (Earl's name got a round of boos), but that it had switched to Russell (more boos).

Maine, Maryland, and Massachusetts seconded Truman, the last through the voice of a lovely creature named Miss Catherine V. Danehy, in a charming black frock and a thick television makeup. But she talked too long, and the gallery, eager to see Truman, grew restless and noisy.

Ladies Powder Noses, Grit Teeth

On the floor the lady politicos powdered their shiny noses and gritted their teeth. And so it went to the dreary end.

Galleries Fill Up Fast

The afternoon session was adjourned to 6:30 P.M., but it was 7 o'clock before Chairman Rayburn clouted the convention to something resembling order. At that time all save a few of the delegates and alternates were in their places, and the galleries were fast filling up.

A Presbyterian pastor in a Palm Beach suit prayed at length and a pretty young woman by the name of Mrs. Cornelius Vanderbilt Whitney was put up to star-spangle the banner. She turned out to have a pleasant voice and was neatly dressed in a simple but expensive-looking evening gown. Around her neck was a double rope of pearls and from her ears glowed clusters of diamonds.

Everyone was impatient to get to the nomination speeches, but a national convention never proceeds in a direct and rational manner. First there must be speeches, always and invariably bad.

Southerners Caucus Diligently

The first bore chosen to harry the poor delegates was Governor Herbert B. Maw (this is his actual name) of Utah. A brisk, bald-headed man in a blue suit, he told how the New Deal had turned billions of cubic miles of water loose upon the deserts of his state, and so saved the Mormon farmers from drought and despair.

While he roared on, the delegates down on the floor prepared for the expected Truman demonstrations. Those of Maine hung a boiled lobster to one of their standards and a huge potato to the other.

The southerners, thrown into the last ditch of Armageddon by proceedings of the afternoon, caucused diligently.

The next noise was Senator Brien McMahon, of Connecticut. When he rose up the band greeted him with "My Wild Irish Rose." He gave over most of his harangue to excoriating old Joe Stalin, and if the crowd had been able to hear him he would probably have evoked resounding roars.

Bellowing Barely Audible

But though he bellowed into the mike in the manner of the Bull of Bashan there was so much disturbance in the hall that he was barely audible from the *Sunpaper's* pew in the press-stand, not 20 feet away.

Rayburn let him howl on without offering to help him. Such rhetoricians are the heroic shock troops of American politics, but when they go gurgling down to oblivion no one mourns them . . .

A number of other whoopers lingered expectantly on the platform, but toward 8 o'clock, with serious business impending, Rayburn presented various minor dignitaries to present formal resolutions.

One authorized the national committee to run the party until the next convention; others thanked Mayor Samuel, of Philadelphia, the newsreel boys, the ushers, and so on for their services; yet another thanked Rayburn himself for presiding with justice and finesse. A few minutes later Alabama staged its walkout and the real show was on.

The Progressives

Mencken And The Swami

Marx, Lenin, Uncle Joe Missing At Convention

PHILADELPHIA, JULY 22—Large portraits of the Swami Wallace and the banjo-player Glen Taylor now hang in the convention hall where those of Truman and FDR hung two weeks ago, and sundry other revisions have been made in the decor.

All the state flags have been taken out, and the United States seal has been removed from the front of the speakers' stand. In place of the latter there is an austere sign reading "Founding Convention of the New Party." Far behind the platform is a long banner reading "Let Us Create a Better America."

But the street-carnival flags and bunting that adorned and glorified both the Republican and Democratic conventions are still in place, and some new banners have been hung from the huge cluster of powerful lights which serves the movie and television boys. On these banners are colossal portraits of Wallace, FDR, Lincoln (without whiskers), Jefferson, and the late George Norris, of Nebraska, along with stimulating quotings from their works.

Their Agents Seem Plentiful

Karl Marx is missing, and so are Lenin and Uncle Joe, but their agents seem to be plentiful in the hosts now assembling. A lot of them were heard by the platform committee today, and others are on the committee itself and also on the rules committee. This boring from within has been denounced somewhat belatedly by the Swami himself, but there is nothing that he can do about it.

This afternoon I met a Socialist in the hall who had a list of the two committees showing the known Communists on them. There were plenty, I assure you. Significantly enough, he could find very few on the arrangements committee, the credentials committee or the nominating committee. The first of these committees has only routine work to do, the second is admitting anyone who doesn't believe in the profit motive, and the third has only a formal existence, for everyone expects, of course, that Wallace and Taylor will be nominated.

Field Day For Rhetoricians

The platform committee met in almost continuous session all day, listening to an almost endless stream of rhetoricians. They spoke for a vast variety of reform organizations, ranging from the Society of American Poets to the Negro Elks, from the Armenian Youth of America to the National Council of Women Chiropractors and from Delta Phi Epsilon to the Ladies of the Grand Army of the Republic.

The Hon. Rexford G. Tugwell, chairman of the committee, heard them cheerfully enough, but certainly not continuously. Ever and anon he slipped out of the unbearably hot hearing room for a breath of air and maybe a spot of Coca Cola. At such time he handed over his gavel to some other member.

Most of these substitutes operated in their shirt-sleeves, with neckties off and collars open. So did nearly all the remaining members. Once, during the long afternoon, I looked up and saw two with their coats on. I record the names of these heroes for posterity. They were the Hon. Reuben Borough and the Hon. Alfred K. Stern.

Tugwell, when on the bridge, warned the speakers against talking too much, but none of them heeded him. One indignant brother, howling against ecclesiastical influence in public affairs, and especially in education, allowed that he represented hundreds of organizations, mustering millions of votes.

Landlords Laugh Deliriously

Another, a gentleman of color, bellered for relief for American artists of all sorts, many of whom he declared on iron rations. He said that among the 50,000 "trained painters, sculptors and graphic artists" in the country the average annual income is but $173, and that among the 60,000 writers, despite the presence of many plutocrats among them, it is only $900.

The convention's public relations staff announced today that many of the incoming delegates expect and demand free quarters for the duration. Unhappily, the party treasurer is unable to pay the board of all of them, and the Philadelphia landlords, mainly Republicans, laugh deliriously at such ideas. But today the staff found at least one Philadelphia woman, a true lover of humanity, who not only offered a room but one actually air-cooled.

Maryland has been moved up to the front of the hall, to the right of the speakers' stand. Only Texas is ahead of it.

Mencken And The Votaries

Sudden Flap Of Wings Would Be No Surprise

PHILADELPHIA, SATURDAY, JULY 24—The customers of the Henry Wallace evangel met last night in the same hard-used hall that lately saw the uproars of the Republicans and Democrats, and there and then organized their new party and prepared in its name to heave Henry into the presidency of this great republic.

No "stop-Wallace" movement has developed among the delegates. He has them all, come hell or high water. To a very large extent he has acquired the semi-celestial character which attached to the late FDR. If, when he is nominated today, he suddenly sprouts wings and begins flapping about the hall, no one will be surprised.

Press-Conference Adventure

At his press conference yesterday afternoon, some journalistic miscreants tried to trap him into admitting that he was an adherent of a society of East Indian magicians and an intimate of a sinister snake charmer known as a Guru. He refused to admit, but he also refused to deny it.

The episode, however, made no more impression on his communicants than if it had been discovered that he had found a nickel on the street or joined the Tall Cedars of Lebanon.

The first session of their convention was not a bad show, though like any other such gathering it had its dull spots. The delegates filled all the space on the floor given over to both delegates and alternates at the two orthodox, or dirt conventions, and the galleries were pretty well crowded.

Despite the infernal heat in the hall, there was a quick and vociferous response to every flash of oratory from the platform, and ever and anon the brethren and sistern leaped from their pens and paraded the aisles.

If the night's proceedings were actually maneuvered by goons of the Kremlin, there was certainly no overt sign of it. The delegates, as seen from the press-stand, looked as little like the Communists of legend as they looked like professional jobholders who packed both the Republican and Democratic conventions.

They were, in the overwhelming main, plain people of the sort who go on the box picnics and believe that a horse hair put into a bottle of water will turn into a snake and that Dr. Townsend's old-age pension plan would reduce the cost of living.

Women Plainly Garbed

The ladies were chiefly bulky and unlovely, precisely like the Republican and Democratic ladies, but they did not run to the same gaudy and preposterous frocks and hats. Instead they were plainly and indeed rather poorly garbed and at least 65 per cent of them wore no hats at all.

The bucks sat in their shirt-sleeves, displaying their suspenders. There were dark faces spotted everywhere in the hall, but it seemed to me that they were fewer than the relative strength of the colored population might have justified. Distinctly Jewish faces were decidedly scarce. I saw no Indians, Chinese, Malays, Eskimos or Arabs.

The parades and other demonstrations were amateurish and despite their heartiness failed altogether to show the technical polish and finish of those managed by the old-party machines. Sometimes two streams of whoopers collided at the head of an aisle; at other times one marched up an aisle and another down the same, and they tangled all along the line.

Notes Banal Placards

The banners and placards they carried were mainly home-made and showed it. Missouri had the only one with any humor in it, to wit: "Missouri wants a big brave man, not a brave little man."

The Maryland delegation confined itself to waving the state flag and holding aloft small placards announcing the habitats of the holders, for example, "Dundalk," "Park Circle," "Essex," "12th Ward," "15th Ward," and so on.

The placards of the other delegations were on the same banal level, for example, "25 electoral votes coming from California" and "Why tarry with Harry?" There seemed to be no very high pressure of ideas in either speakers or hearers. The former simply howled the obvious, and the latter simply howled back. Most of the speakers were third, fourth and ninth rate.

Ring Sparkles With Stones

The exception was the Hon. Charles P. Howard, of Iowa, who intoned the keynote speech. He is a tall, full-bodied barrister of the color of a good ten-cent cigar, and there is an African roll in his voice that is far from unpleasant.

He wore a gray suit, white shirt and a polychrome necktie, and on the third finger of his left hand sparkled a ring set with a handful of stones. I could not get near enough to it to assay it, but if it was real gold set with Class A diamonds, it would be worth at least $175,000.

The Hon. Mr. Howard made a good speech, as speeches ran this evening. It was mainly devoted to excoriating Hitler, the du Ponts, the Rockefellers, Truman and other such malefactors.

All Hitler's chief backers, he said, have now been restored to power in Germany by the Allies, and the outlook for democracy there is worse than it was before the war. In conclusion, Lawyer Howard dropped kind words for Abraham Lincoln, Frederick Douglass, Roger Williams and FDR.

Loud Greeting For Isacson

The loudest welcome of the evening went to the Hon. Leo Isacson, whose election to Congress in the Bronx last autumn was an enormous victory for the Marxian metaphysic. A large number of his friends had come down from New York to give him a friendly hand, and all hands pitched in to help.

It took Comrade Howard fifteen minutes to blast a channel of silence through the hullabaloo for Isacson's speech.

He devoted it largely to an account of a recent trip to Israel. Its high point, he said, was a visit to the venerable Chief Rabbi of Jerusalem, who asked him "How's my old friend Henry Wallace?" He then proceeded to denounce President Truman passionately for continuing the embargo on the shipment of arms to the embattled Jews.

Name Finally Chosen

"The quality of the fighting forces of Israel," he said, "has never been surpassed in the history of the world."

It took the rules committee of the convention three or four days to decide upon a name for the new party. Hitherto it has been known variously as the Wallace party, the New party, and the New Progressive party.

The committee finally decided tonight to chop off the New and call it simply the Progressive party, and when this was reported by the Hon. C.B. Baldwin it was agreed to unanimously and with ecstatic huzzahs.

When this business was concluded and Isacson ceased his roaring, it was a quarter to twelve, and the crowd was beginning to lose its steam.

The gallery was half empty and not a few of the delegates were beginning to shuffle out. Some belated reports of committees, largely formal and unintelligible, converted this flight into a rush, and at 11:58, to a burst of hillbilly music, the first session adjourned.

Orchestra And A Choir

Before the main orgies began, an effort was made to heat up the delegates with song, and to that end an orchestra and a choir had been provided and a battery of gitter-players, banjoists and crooners. This effort did not pan out very well.

The choir, led by Prof. Leonard DePaur, was seated far behind the speakers' stand in a region barely within reach of the loud-speaker system, and the shirt-sleeved band, led by Prof. Hishy Kaye, was directly in front of it.

The trouble was that the two professors could hear only faintly the crooners and bellowers at the mike, and the crooners and bellowers could not hear the choir and orchestra at all. Moreover, the crooners and bellowers were apparently unaware that a crowd always establishes tempo of its own, and pays no attention to leaders.

Singing At Crosspurposes

The result was a considerable confusion. "John Brown's Body" went on at one tempo in the choir and orchestra, at another among the delegates, and at still a third at the mike.

After a while this cacophanous discrepancy was somewhat smoothed out, but never quite sufficiently.

The choir, numbering perhaps 60, consisted of both whites and blacks, males and females, and its leader was a colored man. The orchestra was all white, and the crooners were all of the same color.

Of the latter the principal performer was Peter Seeger, who led "The Star-Spangled Banner" in circus time and then flabbergasted those who were trying to catch up with him by busting into the second stanza.

Clergyman Says Prayer

Inasmuch as not more than a dozen persons in the hall knew its words, the best they could do was to hum along. When he shut down, a clergyman was put up to pray. The Republicans and Democrats both had Cardinal Dougherty for this office, and he appeared in his gorgeous robes. But the New party was content with a Protestant dominie in a neat gray business suit. He prayed a good deal longer than His Eminence, and apparently with more confidence.

The orchestra consisted of 6 saxophones, 4 trumpets, 2 sliphorns, a tuba, a piano, a harmonium and drums. A bull-fiddle was lying in a corner, but no one appeared to play it.

Mencken At Hall And Park

Sees Comrades Emerge And Wallace Nominated Day

PHILADELPHIA, JULY 24—After lurking in the catacombs and sewers of the hall for three days, the Communists sneaked into the main arena or Cave of Adullam (1 Samuel 22:1,2)* this morning, and put the innocent delegates to the Wallace convention over the barrel.

Tonight the rules of the New party are precisely what they wanted them to be, and their trusted stooges are sitting on almost every salient stool in the party organization.

The Communists are old hands at such tricks, and get away with them almost infallibly. First they horn into places on the important committees, then they frame the reports thereof after the other members have fallen asleep or gone home, and then they come in and bull the reports through in a din of words.

Maryland Challenge Beaten

They have worked this game in the labor unions for years, including many unions that have formally repudiated them and denounced them as enemies to the flag. They did it once more this morning, though most of the delegates in the hall probably didn't know what was going on.

The Maryland delegation, speaking through the Hon. James S. Martin, challenged one of these maneuvers, to wit, a scheme to jam through a rule designed to give the inner circle, probably to be Communist dominated, authority to pack the national committee with additional members, chosen God knows how or by whom.

Martin argued against this Stalinist plan appositely and eloquent-

*David therefore departed thence, and escaped to the cave of Adullam: and when his brethren and all his father's house heard it, they went down thither to him.

And everyone that was in distress, and everyone that was in debt, and everyone that was discontented, gathered themselves unto him; and he became a captain over them; and there were with him about four hundred men.

ly, and he got some support from Massachusetts, Illinois and Michigan, but in ten minutes his protest was talked to death by virtuosi of the party line, and the rule was adopted with a whoop.

Platform Manipulation

Several other revolutionists made attempts on other rules, but always with the same result. Orators almost without number deafened the delegates with their bellows, and the bosses on the platform manipulated the flow of motions and countermotions with such skill that everything went through as planned.

All of these bosses, of course, are not Communists, at least officially. Many of them, in fact, have frequently belabored communism in high, astounding terms.

But each and every one of them is a faithful dues-paying member of the "I am not a Communist,but—" association, founded by the late Heywood Broun of blessed memory, and they are always ready with their poniards and shillelaghs when work is to be done for the holy cause.

Learned Book By Heart

The current president of this great philanthropic association is the Hon. Albert Fitzgerald, permanent chairman of the convention. He looks like the twenty-third vice-president of a New York trust company, and he has all the gift for non-Euclidean mathematics that goes with that high office, but he is actually an old-time labor stiff, and long since learned the book by heart.

The phosphorescent revolts of the morning were not serious and putting them down was child's play, but the bosses apparently feared that if the delegates once escaped from the rhetorical and parliamentary miasmas in the hall they might plot some major deviltry in the open air.

In consequence, the first session was stretched out until there was only half an hour left before the nominating session began at 2 P.M.

No Worse Than Other Two

This nominating session was a dull and dreadful affair, but certainly no worse than those staged at the Republican and Democratic conventions. Despite the fact that there was not even the shadow of a contest, the whoopers who performed on the platform or from the floor managed to get more or less drama into their vociferations, and there were frequent roars of applause.

Several times the proceedings were halted for demonstrations, and that which began when Wallace's name was formally introduced by the Hon. Fred Stover ran nearly half an hour.

The speakers, including Stover, were nearly all hams. They were talking, not for the audience before them, but for the radio and television fans back home, and so their howling was adapted to the mike, not to the vastness of the hall.

Colored Shouters Better

Some of these crooners were white and some were colored. On the whole, the colored shouters were better than the pale-faces and got and deserved more plaudits.

The best of all was the Hon. Goldie Watson, of Philadelphia, who delivered the 77 votes of Pennsylvania. She turned out to be a good-looking brown young woman in very becoming black clothes, and she spoke in a clear and pleasant voice. If she had not gone on a shade too long, she would have been the star of the afternoon show.

The disease afflicted most of the other speakers. They bawled for what lay closest to their hearts, and forgot all the other paths to Utopia.

Each Has His Target

The colored brethren denounced segregation, the Jews demanded arms for Israel, the union boys execrated Wall Street, the southern white leaders (a very small band) shouted that they could take care of themselves without the aid of either the Ku Klux Klan or the federal army, and so on.

Texas took time to revile Pappy O'Daniel and Tom Clark, and Rhode Island announced the doom of its two senators, both of whom were described as millionaires.

Fitzgerald warned the delegates that Wallace and Taylor were expected in the hall before the end of the afternoon, and that if the flow of oratory was not abated there would be no time to feast eyes on them, but the windjammers kept on and on. Not more than one or two states failed to send up bores to second the nomination of the Swami. Even the District of Columbia, Hawaii and Puerto Rico joined in the din.

. . . And Night

PHILADELPHIA, JULY 24—Henry Wallace and Glen Taylor, nominated for president and vice-president this afternoon by the third boiling of the so-called Progressive party, to the tune of such frenzied rhetoric that strong men paled and shook, were notified of the fact at Shibe Park tonight.

Shibe Park is the headquarters of the American League Athletics, and today the team picked up so much animal magnetism from the impending orgies that they walloped the Detroit Tigers and went to first place in the league.

This cosmic battle left the ball park somewhat scarred and mangy, and in the evening it got a further curry combing from the exultant Progressives.

Second Base Speakers' Stand

A speakers' stand had been erected off second base, and on the sandy wastes to each side of it were accommodations for the radio and television (left) and a choir and band (right).

The park is so large that, even with loud-speakers operating at 700 amperes, the band could not fill it, and sometimes the choir was not heard at all. When the band cut loose at 8 P.M., on time to the second, the stands got the sombre grunt of the tuba, and an occasional sigh of the sliphorns, but the saxophones might as well have been blowing in Baltimore.

The convention banjo-player (not Taylor himself, but Comrade Seeger, a very superior artist), fared much better. Having had plenty of radio experience he hugged the mike on the stand, and as a result his plucking of his strings had the effect of a series of blows with an ax.

Following the Marxist ideology the spectators were charged for their seats, and it was hoped to raise enough thereby to pay for the whole convention. The scale ranged from 25 cents for students penned in the left-field bleachers to $2.60 for Wall Street spies in the grandstand behind the plate.

Unhappily, not enough fans showed up to fill all the seats, and such spectators as had laid in sheafs of tickets were left with a bitter foretaste of the impending depression. Five female cheerleaders had been provided to heat up the students, but they achieved no effects that could be described as electrical.

These preliminaries to the main exercises, in fact, were pretty dismal, and coming after the enormous uproars in the convention hall this afternoon they seemed almost stealthy.

False Starts And Stage Waits

It was not until the Hon. Sam Wanamaker, a movie actor, called the meeting to order at 8:40, nearly three-quarters of an hour late, that there was anything for the crowd to get its teeth into.

Even so there were false starts and stage-waits and it was not until 9 o'clock that the first scheduled speaker, the Hon. Joseph B. Rainey, of Philadelphia, was introduced.

His Honor is a man of color, and aspires to desert jurisprudence for a seat in Congress. He spoke too judicially and briefly to inflame the crowd, but the next speaker, the Hon. Vito Marcantonio, the American Labor party congressman from New York, soon had it bellowing.

This was Marcantonio's third speech before the New party convention, and all of them have been loud and alarming. When waves of applause drowned him out he kept on roaring and waving his arms. His discourse was mainly devoted, not to whooping up the new party, but to defending the Communists.

Robeson Follows Marcantonio

When efforts are made to put them down, he said, the thin line between democracy and fascism is obliterated. This calamity can only be staved off, he concluded, by electing Wallace and Taylor.

The fiery Vito was succeeded by the Hon. Paul Robeson, the Negro baritone. Hitherto Robeson has contributed his mite to Utopian science by singing songs, principally "Old Man River," but this time he chose to make a speech, and he made a very good one.

His powerful voice, greatly magnified by the loud-speaker system, rang through the ball field like the roll of artillery, and what he had to say about the villainies of Truman and Dewey was couched in simple and effective English.

Song About Underprivileged

Having got off his speech he resumed song by plunging into a lugubrious hymn about the hardships of the underprivileged. As he sang he cupped his right hand over his right ear, apparently in an effort to protect it from the deafening kickback from the loud-speakers.

Following this, he sang a parody of "Glory, Glory, Hallelujah" to words beginning "Marching On With Henry Wallace." The crowd attempted to join in the chorus and to keep time by clapping hands, but he did not encourage this assistance; and when he finished he about-faced at once and marched from the stage.

Robeson's runner-up was the Hon. William Gailmor, one of the mystery men of the Wallace entourage. He has been denounced violently by the press agents of Wall Street and accused of various delinquencies, but Wallace seems to have great confidence in him, probably because he is a highly accomplished money-raiser.

Money-Raising Show

Tonight he put on a show like those made familiar years ago by such old-time evangelists as Billy Sunday. First, describing eloquently the need for radio money in the campaign, he called for contributions of $1,000 each—and got perhaps a dozen of them.

Then he reduced the ante to $500, but the checks began to come in more slowly.

To encourage liberality he launched into a bitter denunciation of what he called the hatchet press, and said that it had been carrying on a hellish conspiracy of defamation against Wallace during the convention. This needled the customers, and during the next half hour they sent up many more pledges for $1,000, $500, $250, $200, $100, and what have you.

Dollar-Waving For Television

He had a troop of cuties to circulate in the stands, lifting pledges, checks and cash.

Finally, when the law of diminishing returns began to squeeze him, he asked those who could not afford any more to chip in $1 each, and when even the flow of dollar bills petered out he asked the holdouts to wave dollar bills, that the scene might be embalmed by television.

All this took a lot of time and it was 10:30 before the vice-presidential candidate, Senator Taylor, got to the platform. His reception was hearty, but not prolonged. He had a speech prepared, but prefaced it with some ad-libbing, chiefly devoted to describing how he had formerly been afraid to speak at pro-Soviet meetings but had lately got over it.

No Zip Or Zowie In It

His formal speech must be set down as a very feeble effort, and it got relatively little applause. There was no zip or zowie in it. Coming after the incandescent oratory of this afternoon, it seemed sophomoric, not to say, sophomoronic.

But at its conclusion his wife, his children and his brother were beckoned to the platform, and he made up for his failure as an orator by singing "When You Were Sweet Sixteen" with them in an exaggerated barber-shop manner.

It was a bad performance, but there was some humor in it, and the crowd was delighted.

By this time it was 11 o'clock, and the Hon Albert J. Fitzgerald appeared at the mike to introduce Wallace.

Enter The Hero Of The Evening

Just as the magic name was pronounced the candidate himself appeared athwart the home-plate in a shiny open car, accompanied by Taylor and the ladies of their families.

When the car proceeded to a leisurely circling of the field, with photographers clambering over it, admirers following and shoving it, and a squad of Philadelphia police howling, leaping about and waving their arms, the crowd broke into the first really noisy demonstration of the evening.

It started as a banal parade of the sort that go on in convention halls, but in a few minutes a couple of hundred youngsters jumped into the field, clasped hands in a long line, and were presently whooping around the infield in a sort of snake-dance. It was silly but it was somehow charming, and while it went on, with the rest of the crowd chanting "We Want Wallace," the hero of the evening had to wait by the mike.

Poor Swami At Least Desists

He had been booked to take his stance there at 10:30, but it was now almost an hour later. His speech, which is reported elsewhere, was mainly devoted to denouncing Truman for his failure to fall in with the ideas of the Russians. It naturally pleased the comrades and fellow-travelers who swarmed in the stands, but it was so badly designed and so badly delivered that it offered very little provocation to hullabaloo.

After he had gone on for less than half an hour, the crowd began to filter out. The weather, which had been infernally hot, suddenly turned cool tonight, and in the press box toward midnight it was actually chilly. Eventually the poor Swami, his voice much worn, humanely desisted.

Mencken Tastes The Cake

Finds Several Raisins In Paranoiac Confection

PHILADELPHIA, JULY 25—After another long and dismal day of pathological rhetoric relieved only by the neat and amusing operations of the party-line steamroller, the delegates to the founding convention of the third and maybe last Progressive party, began shuffling off for home tonight.

On the whole, the show has been good, as such things go in the Republic. It has provided no sharp and gory conflict of candidates like that which marked the Republican convention. It has offered no brutal slaughter of a minority like that which pepped up the Democratic convention, but it has at least brought together a large gang of picturesque characters, and it has given everyone a clear view of its candidates and its platform.

No Access Of Dignity

The former certainly do not emerge from it with anything properly describable as an access of dignity. Wallace started off by making a thumping ass of himself in his preliminary press conference, and did nothing to redeem himself by his bumbling and boresome delivery of his speech of acceptance (otherwise not a bad one) last night.

As for Taylor, he has made it plain to all that there is nothing to him whatever save a third-rate mountebank from the great open spaces, a good deal closer to Pappy O'Daniel than to Savonarola. Soak a radio clown for ten days and ten nights in the rectified juices of all the cow-state Messiahs ever heard of, and you have him to the life. Save on the remotest fringes of the intellectually underprivileged it is highly unlikely that he will add anything to the strength of the new party.

That Guru Matter

Wallace's imbecile handling of the Guru matter revealed a

stupidity that is hard to fathom. He might have got rid of it once and for all by simply answering yes or no, for no one really cares what foolishness he fell for ten or twelve years ago.

He is swallowing much worse doses of hokum at this minute, and no complaint is heard. But he tried disingenuously to brush off the natural and proper questions of the journalists assembled, and when they began to pin him down and press him he retreated into plain nonsense.

Worst, he had begun this sorry exhibition by a long and witless tirade against the press. He went into the conference with every assumption in his favor. He came out of it tattered and torn.

The convention naturally attracted swarms of crackpots of all sorts and for three days and three nights they did their stuff before the sweating platform committee, ostensibly headed by the cynical Rexford Tugwell.

Platform Defended On Floor

But the platform was actually drawn up by the Communists and fellow-travelers on the committee, and when it got to the floor this afternoon they protected it waspishly and effectively against every raid from more rational quarters.

When an honest but humorless Yankee from Vermont tried to get in a plank disclaiming any intention to support the Russian assassins in every eventuality, no matter how outrageous their doings, it was first given a hard parliamentary squeeze by the Moscow fuglemen on the platform and then bawled to death on the floor.

Now Out On Top

No one who has followed the proceedings can have any doubt that the Communists have come out on top. Wallace, a little while back, was declaring piously that he didn't want their support, but certainly made no effort to brush it off during the convention.

In any case, his effort to climb from under, like Eleanor Roosevelt's, came far too late, and no person of any common sense took it seriously.

A Bucket Of Bones

As for Taylor, he has been cultivating the Kremlin, openly and without apology, all week, and the comrades in attendance seem to have no doubt of his fealty. When he got up in Shibe Park to make his so-called speech of acceptance—an effort worthy of a corn doctor at a county fair—he actually held it up long enough to throw them a bucket of bones.

The delegates, taking them one with another, have seemed to me to be of generally low intelligence but it is easy to overestimate the idiocy of the participants in such mass paranoias.

People of genuine sense seldom come to them, and when they do come they are not much heard from. I believe that the percentage of downright half-wits has been definitely lower than in, say, the Democratic convention of 1924, and not much higher than in the Democratic convention of this year.

Old Types Persist

This is not saying, of course, that there were not plenty of psychopaths present. They rolled in from North, East, South and West, and among them were all of the types listed by Emerson in his description of the Chandos Street convention of reformers, in Boston more than a century ago.

Such types persist, and they do not improve as year chases year. They were born with believing minds, and when they are cut off by death from believing in an FDR they turn inevitably to such Rosicrucians as poor Henry.

The more extreme varieties, I have no doubt, would not have been surprised if a flock of angels had swarmed down from Heaven to help whoop him up, accompanied by the red dragon with seven heads and ten horns described in Revelation XII, 3. Alongside these feeble-minded folk were gangs of dubious labor leaders, slick Communists, obfuscators, sore veterans, Bible belt evangelists, mischievous college students, and such-like old residents of the Cave of Adullum.

But it would be unfair to forget the many quite honest, and even reasonably intelligent folk, male and female, who served as raisins in the cake. Some of them I recalled seeing years ago at other gatherings of those born to hope. They were veterans of many and many now-forgotten campaigns to solve the insoluble and remedy the irremediable.

They followed Bryan in their day, and TR and the elder La Follette and all the other roaring magicians of recent history. They are survivors of Populism, the Emmanuel movement, the no-more-scrub-bulls agitation, the ham-and eggs crusade of Upton Sinclair, the old-age pension frenzy of Dr. Francis Townsend, the share-the-wealth gospel of Huey Long, and so on without end.

Truman Main Target

They are grocery-store economists, moony professors in one-building "universities," editors of papers with no visible circulation, preachers of lost evangels, customers of a hundred schemes to cure all the sorrows of the world.

Whether they will muster enough votes on Election Day to make a splash remains to be seen. In the United States new parties usually do pretty well at the start, and then fade away. Judging by the speeches they listen to here in Philadelphia their principal current devil is the embattled gents furnisher, Harry S. Truman. I heard very little excoriation of Dewey, but they screamed against Harry at every chance.

IV
The Campaign

Home To Roost

Mencken Calls Dixie Chickens 'Spavined'

AUGUST 1*—The gallant Confederates who attempted a raid upon the late Democratic National Convention got a bad licking on the floor, but that licking did not dispose of them, nor even seriously punish them. What ails them now is a double handicap, both halves of it of southern origin. The first is to be found in the fact that when they got home all the worst frauds in the South rushed up to kiss them and have since hung about their necks. The second half springs out of the general northern assumption, unhappily well supported by recent history, that whatever originates in the South is half-idiotic, and hardly deserves to be heard.

That assumption is bitterly resented by enlightened southerners, but the record is the record. The South, for years past, has been a sewer of imbecility. It has supported every major aberration, whether political or social, that has afflicted the country, and it has supported most of them with a degree of enthusiasm bordering on the delirious. I name the Bryan madness. I name Prohibition. I name Fundamentalism. I name the New Deal. I name the Anti-Al Smith and Huey Long uproars. I name the two wars to make the world safe for democracy.

But there is no need to labor the list, for it would be hard to think of any lunacy that doesn't belong on it. Time was when the South, perhaps more than any other section of the country, was fertile in ideas, but even more fertile in first-rate men. But at least since the eighties, nine-tenths of the so-called ideas that it has produced have been silly, and nine-tenths of the leaders shabby and preposterous fellows. When the last of its Civil War heroes died it went underground, intellectually speaking, and there it has remained ever since, entertaining the civilized world with such frightful burlesques

---

*Mencken wrote subsequent pieces from his home office in Baltimore.

of civilization as the Scopes trial, the Leo Frank lynching, and the share-the-wealth hubbub.

The result today is that the Dixiecrat movement is getting a great deal less sober attention than it deserves. It looks, from across the Potomac and Ohio, like nothing more than a fresh pestilence of Longs, Bilbos, Tillmans, Bleases, Talmadges and Pappy O'Daniels. It is, in fact, nothing of the sort, whatever the excrescences that now burden it. It is fundamentally quite as serious in purpose, and quite as rational, as any other regional movement that has appeared in recent years, and some of its leaders are worthy of the highest respect. Certainly it would be absurd to dismiss such men as Governor J. Strom Thurmond, of South Carolina, and former Governor Dan Moody, of Texas, as windbags of the common sort. They are men of intelligence and they are men of honor, and when they take to the bush it is safe to assume that they have a genuine grievance.

The colored brother, it seems to me, is hardly more than a bystander in the combat, though he will be injured no matter what the issue. If the embattled Confederates throw Truman and company off he will see a halt in the process of liberation that has been going on for some years, with the best class of southerners supporting it. And if the damyankee politicians, with their eyes upon the Harlem vote, push their drastic "reforms" through, he will be the chief victim of the ensuing revival of Reconstruction.

It is this threat of another dismal dose of Reconstruction that chiefly alarms the more intelligent southerners. They are painfully aware of what went on in the seventies, and they are naturally fearful of a repetition, with northerner jobholders, most of them dishonest and nearly all of them jackasses, substituted for the carpetbaggers of the first canto. They believe that they have some civil rights, too, and they are resolved not only to protect those that remain but to regain those that have been already lost to New Deal totalitarianism. They hope to do it peacefully by an appeal to Article X of the Bill of Rights, but if that appeal fails they are willing to try stronger medicines.

I must confess that I sympathize with them, despite my life-long devotion to exposing their deficiences. It must be manifest that if the whole program of the Yankee messiahs, by the Force Bill of 1890 out of the Communist Manifesto, is put through with any vigor, life will become almost impossible in large areas of the South, and a third Bull Run will begin casting its shadows before.

But the position of the intelligent southerners, as I have observed, is greatly weakened by the stupidity of the South as a whole. Having supported the New Deal violently for sixteen years, and profited enormously by its reckless looting of the North, including Maryland, it can't complain now that the North is preparing to give it a poisonous dose out of the same black bottle. It is not possible to play the idiot for years on end and then suddenly turn Aristotle. It is not possible to wallow in the buncombe of Long, Bilbo, Pepper, Lister Hill, O'Daniel and the like until all the stomachs north of the Potomac begin to turn and then appeal to reason behind a façade of Thurmonds, Moodys and Harry Byrds.

The South had its chance to come out for intelligence a long while ago. Instead it turned to Bryan, Tom Watson, Prohibition, Fundamentalism and the Ku Klux Klan. It is now paying the devastating penalty. Its spavined and bedraggled chickens are coming home to roost.

Mencken Probes Mystery

Is Wallace A Goon Or Sucker? He Asks

AUGUST 4—The anatomy and physiology of the new Progressive party, examined in the calm of the laboratory, begin to take on a certain mystery, not unlike that steeping the Swami Wallace himself.

Is he actually a goon of Moscow or only a sucker? My own impression, I should say at once, is that he is the latter, but I should add that it would not surprise me greatly to hear that his infatuation with Uncle Joe has gone a good deal further than a mere long-distance flirtation.

Certainly, it is impossible to imagine him being unaware of the bold and cynical manner in which the Marxians collared control of his New party. He was there to see the operation for himself, and if, perchance, he was blind to it, then there were plenty of other persons on hand to tell him.

There was, indeed, nothing occult about the process. It was almost as public as an old-time lynching in Mississippi. Under lights of at least 500,000 candlepower and in the presence of 15,000 spectators, the Marxian brethren took over the late convention in Philadelphia. They had all the important committees packed with trusted agents, and more agents appeared in all important places on the platform.

Every attempt from the floor to get some saving grace into the proceedings was voted down with raucous roars. No one who showed the slightest suspicion of Uncle Joe or the shadow of an idea there was a case against him, was given a fair hearing, or even, in fact, any hearing at all. If the sessions of the convention had been held in the Bronx or the London School of Economics, or in the Kremlin itself, they could not have differed materially from the obscene show staged in Republican Philadelphia.

Now that it is over, and sober second thoughts have begun to work, some of the less *mashuggah* delegates have begun to deny all this, but their denials are so thin that they are quite laughable. If the Communists were not in control, who was? Surely not the surviving powers and principalities of the New Deal, for the only one of them plainly visible was the Hon. Rexford G. Tugwell, Ph.D., Litt. D., and Tugwell was shunted to the shooting-cellars so fast that all I could hear from him at the finish was a sepulchral groan.

Not one of Wallace's old associates in the cabinet showed up, nor any of his former aides in the killing of pigs and fattening of gimmie farmers. Jimmie Roosevelt was not there, though he seems to go everywhere that photographers assemble, nor was his venerable Ma. A great many party-line labor racketeers were on hand, and some were on the platform, but there was not one among them whose name would have been familiar to the great masses of the plain people. I saw only two congressmen—both of them faithful hewers to the party line from uptown New York City, which is quite outside the United States. The only senator present was the candidate for vice-president—a wholly preposterous ham from the wilds of Idaho.

And in the hall? In the hall, alas, even the Marxians were nonentities, and I encountered only one of enough importance to have gone through the wringer of the Thomas committee. He was, he told me, booked for three months in jail, and he lamented the fact lugubriously, though I tried to cheer him by recalling Socrates, John Bunyan and Al Capone.

The delegates were nearly all obscure characters, and most of them were more or less mysterious. The celebrated wreckers of Wall Street who swarmed at previous Progressive conventions were simply not there. I spent two days and two nights trying to find General Jacob Coxey, but the sergeant-at-arms returned him *non est*. In the Maryland delegation (and likewise in many another delegation) the amalgamated public eminence of all the members was hardly equal to that of a reasonably popular police sergeant.

These were the poor fish that the Marxian sheepmen chased up hill and down dale. Of their good faith I have no doubt, at least if the more nefarious labor leaders be excepted, but of their common sense it is difficult to speak with any assurance. They looked and acted dumb to me, and on the question of dumbness I presume to a certain modest expertness, for I have attended political conventions since 1904, and have included in them Sanhedrins of the customers of Dr. Townsend, Father Coughlin and Gerald Smith, and also a couple of Youth Congresses.

Two problems now entertain the judicious. First is, why didn't Comrade Wallace scare up a more seemly gang? The second is, why did he let the Communists reduce his show to so dreadful an absurdity? As I have said, it is hard for me to believe that he has fallen for the Marxian whim-wham himself, though the historian must not forget that, in the recent past, he fell for the necromancy of Roosevelt II and also for that of Dr. Nicholas Roerich, the Riverside drive snake-charmer. But Roosevelt, at his worst, was a good deal more plausible than the Comintern, and Roerich was a magician and may have fetched poor Henry with malicious animal magnetism.

Has the Kremlin, then, put him on its pay roll, as it has apparently put so many other "trained experts" at Washington? Is he in receipt, every week, of a million rubles for his campaign fund, and a keg of vodka and a carboy of caviare for himself? I simply can't imagine it. So long as he has Comrade Gailmor to sweat the crowd he will have all the campaign fund he needs, and so long as he remains an Iowan he will prefer buttermilk to vodka and hog meat to caviare.

There remains only the theory adumbrated in the second paragraph of this monody, to wit, that the hon. gentleman is a bloody ijjit. It is hard to think this of a candidate for the highest secular office in the sidereal universe (though it has been thought and suggested about others), but it seems to me that one is thrown into its jaws every time one gives the problem prayerful consideration. How else is one to account for the ease with which the Kremlin boys knocked him off? Where else is there an answer to his choice of a small-time mountebank for his running mate? On what other theory are his dismal doings at his low-comedy press conference to be explained, or his speeches?

Truman And Herring

Mencken Meditates On Great Red Hunt

AUGUST 8—The Hon. Mr. Truman's discovery that the investigation of Communist jobholders now going on in Washington is no more than a red herring drawn across the road of his legislative program—this is of a piece with all the other puerile whim-wham that he has been unloading upon the customers of late.

The inquiry he denounces has actually been going on for long months, and even years, and there is no evidence whatsoever that its purpose has changed since it began. That purpose is simply to snout out the Marxians who got on the public pay roll in New Deal days, and have been fighting ever since against the effort to shed them.

What has Dr. Truman contributed to that effort? Absolutely nothing. On the contrary, he has used the great and singular powers of his high office, persistently and relentlessly, to protect them. At this moment a great deal of evidence against them, accumulated diligently by the army, the navy, the FBI and other agencies, is impounded at his order. He alone is responsible for the fact that the congressional committees can't get it.

Why he has taken this strange course I do not know, and can only guess. It would certainly be absurd to conclude that the Kremlin has fetched him, or even that he has joined the "I am not a Communist, but—" association. A yokel from Missouri is not likely to take either route, though here it must not be forgotten that the Hon. Earl Browder is a yokel from Kansas.

Much more plausible, it seems to me, is the theory that what animates him is simply loyalty to the New Deal school tie. He knows very well, if he knows anything at all, that the public offices, in the heyday of Roosevelt II, swarmed with Reds, and he also knows that it was Roosevelt II who, both living and dying, bounced him into the White House. He doesn't want to do anything now, or consent to anything, likely to cast a glare of infamy upon his illustrious Author, and, being far from astute, he takes the method of protecting the worst scoundrels in the Roosevelt entourage.

Such witless loyalty is not unprecedented in his history. He was also a beneficiary, in his day, of a gang of political rogues and vagabonds almost as bad as the Roosevelt gang, to wit, the Pendergast outfit in Kansas City. No one, to this moment, has ever heard him say a word against these criminals. Instead, he has shielded and nursed them, in season and out of season, by every means within his power, both as senator and as president. When he has been heard of on the subject at all, it has been as the bitter implacable enemy, hitting below the belt as well as above, of the decent Missourians who were trying to get them into jail.

Loyalty, at best, is a highly dubious virtue, but when it is carried to so pathological an extreme it becomes a downright vice. More, it becomes foolish. Truman's grotesque endeavor to save the Pendergast gangsters surely did not bull his stock among sensible men; it actually made sensible men hold their noses. And his current services to the Moscow agents who are at last being pulled into the light is having the same effect precisely.

A lot has been made of the fact that the committees engaged in smoking out these rascals have carried on their operations in a generally inept and incompetent manner, and have occasionally knocked some bark off a presumably innocent man. But the number of such cases has been greatly overestimated by the bogus "liberals" who are always so ready to slide down the pole when Reds sound the alarm, and it would probably be hard to get together an authentic list of half a dozen of them all told.

In any such investigation, with the powerful influence of the president thrown on the side of the culprits, it is naturally difficult to get at all the facts, and a good many of those facts, when they come to the surface at last, are encased in thick shrouds of hooey. But it seems to me that the committees, though burdened with manifest idiots, have done, on the whole, a good job, and that every rational man must hope that they will keep on until Truman is booted out of the White House and their hands are untied. What a really competent prosecutor could dredge up, confining himself to the old Labor Relations Board alone, must be a theme of speculation among jail wardens every time they meet for a few drinks.

As for the innocents gored by the committee oxen, I refuse to waste any tears on them. No one holds their misadventure against them, and it seldom does them any harm. Here I speak by the book, for I was myself one of them in the first great Red hunt, following World War I, and stand listed to this day as an agent of Moscow in the celebrated Mrs. Elizabeth Dilling's handbook, "The Red Network."

I am quite unaware of any damage, either contemporaneously or now. A good many people looked at me askance for a while, but they were all people I was glad to be shed of. Forty or 50 lawyers advised me suggestively that I had good grounds for a libel suit against la Dilling, but I have long followed the dogma that no one can libel me, and I saw no reason to depart from it to harass a stupid old woman from Chicago.

Well, with what result? With the result that there is probably not a single man, woman or child on earth today who believes seriously that I am a guzzler of the Marxian hooch, or ever have been. I have been purged and purified like Shadrack, Meshach and Abednego, and feel no worse for it than they did. Age, unhappily, has rusted my withers, but I am still sassy and complacent, and still disliked by genuine Communists and their stooges.

It will be so, too, with the other innocents—if they are actually innocent. But I predict rough sledding for the brethren caught with the goods. If poor Truman slides down the chute on November 2, his successor, alas, will probably be the Hon. Thomas E. Dewey—and Dewey is a hard, harsh man, with long experience in putting salt on the tails of persons who subscribe to anti-social ideologies.

Mencken On The Red Blight

Finds Truman's Remedy Too Little And Too Late

AUGUST 22—On November 16, 1933, the United States Government, by the hand of the late Roosevelt II *selig*, recognized the present government of Russia. On the same day the Hon. Maxim Litvinov, then Soviet commissar of foreign affairs, affixed his hand and seal to the following formal pledge:

> The Soviet Government pledges itself to refrain from the dissemination of propaganda against the political or social order of the United States, or attempting in any way to overthrow American institutions, and to restrain any agency under direct or indirect Soviet control from interfering with the internal affairs of the country.

Again on the same day the Hon. Mr. Litvinov handed to the Hon. Cordell Hull, secretary of state, the following reiteration and amplification of these promises:

> It will be the fixed policy of the Government of the U.S.S.R. . . . to respect scrupulously the indisputable right of the United States to order its own life within its own jurisdiction in its own way, and to refrain from interfering in any manner in the internal affairs of the United States, its territories or possessions; to restrain all persons in Government service and all organizations of the Government or under its direct or indirect control, including organizations in receipt of any financial assistance from it, from any act overt or covert liable in any way whatsoever to injure the tranquility, prosperity, order or security of the whole or any part of the United States.

Whether or not Roosevelt accepted these specific and categorical pledges with his tongue in his cheek I do not pretend to say; but certainly the record is clear that they have never been kept, and that no effort whatsoever has been made to keep them.

Before the end of 1934 the public offices in Washington were swarming with Communists and fellow-travelers, some of them in very high stations, and before the end of 1935 Earl Browder, then the general secretary of the party in the United States, was reporting to Moscow that it was making a vigorous drive for members, that it was preparing to launch a great strike among seamen and longshoremen on the Pacific coast, and that large plans were afoot to horn into unions of other workers and to "take advantage of discontent to create a united proletarian front of workers and farmers."

In June, 1936, the Communists held a national convention in New York, nominated Browder for president, and sent "revolutionary greetings" to the Comintern in Moscow and to the Communist party in Puerto Rico. At the same convention Browder reported that there were already 15,000 Communists in the American trade unions, and that many of them were in key places.

This was a little more than twelve years ago. Certainly no man of any sense will argue that the Moscow boys have abated their operations since, or that those operations have become any the less menacing to "the tranquility, prosperity, order or security of the United States."

The exact contrary has been the case, pledges or no pledges, and everyone knows it. In war and in peace, by direct action and through stooges in false-faces, they have carried on a desperate and relentless effort to destroy the American "political and social order," and to that end no device or expedient has been too devious or dishonorable.

What the cost has been no man can calculate. Strikes fomented by Communists have always been excessively vicious and destructive. It is seldom that there is one without rough-house, and sometimes a great many persons are injured and even killed. The long-drawn-out Allis-Chalmers strike in the upper Middle West offered a good example, and the late strike at an Ohio lens plant offered another. In all such cases the good of the worker is the last thing the Marxian agents care for. Their primary aim is always the promotion of bitter hatreds, for it is their theory that splitting the American people into warring groups is the best way to bring on the brummagem revolution they dream of.

The more intelligent labor leaders are well aware of this purpose, and have made earnest efforts to rid their unions of the Communist infection. But this is not easy, for when a flagrant Red is heaved out, two or more pussyfoots sneak in, and in a little while the whole process of poisoning is resumed. There are very few unions that are actually purged at this moment, and there are even fewer that will stay purged for any length of time. The members of a union, like any other large body of men, are mainly suckers, and it is thus easy to fool them and fetch them.

To say that they are suckers, of course, is simply to say that they are good Americans, for believing what is palpably not true seems to be the hallmark of the people of this great free republic, the envy and despair of all other states. But to set them down as sheer idiots would probably be going too far. They have on occasion responded to more or less enlightened leadership in the past, and they might do it again today.

But, as things stand, they simply haven't got it. The official head of the state, the Hon. Mr. Truman, seems determined to do as little as possible to embarrass or offend the Communists.

If he had to act at last when they set up a kidnapping gang in New York he deserves no credit, for he made no move whatever against all their antecedent malefactions. And in the face of the multiplying and notorious evidence of their effort to overturn the "political and social order of the United States" he has thrown the mantle of his vast power and influence around their American stooges and dupes.

It would be difficult to imagine a more grotesque situation. That it has its humors I do not deny. But it is hard for me to believe that either the American people or Truman himself will do much laughing on November 2.

Mencken Hears Wallace

Finds No Eggs, No Tomatoes, No Excuse For Enthusiasm

SEPTEMBER 13—No one threw an egg or a tomato at Henry Wallace last night but neither did any one show any sign of being fevered by him. It would be hard to imagine a speech falling flatter. He read it in a dull, conversational tone that simply offered no excuse for enthusiasm.

Now and then, to be sure, there was a flutter of applause, but even that happened infrequently. His air was that of a tired professor intoning a worn-out lecture to a room full of students who were half asleep and half dotty.

It was, on the whole, a good audience, though anything but large. Divided about half and half between whites and colored folk, it was plainly made up of serious and respectable people. They listened attentively if not avidly, but there was simply nothing in the hon. gentleman's remarks to lift them.

Local "Malefactors" Cited

Even when he assayed to haul the hides off various local malefactors—for example, the Bethlehem Steel Company, Senator Tydings and Glenn L. Martin—he did it so gently, indeed so weakly, that there was nothing for the customers to get their teeth into.

The high point of his harangue came when he mentioned the Park Board's recent action against mixed tennis matches, and called upon any of its victims who might be present to come to the platform.

Fourteen filed up, and stood behind him looking rather uneasy while he made a few extemporaneous remarks on the subject. But the applause they got was far less than riotous, and his own gloss on their heroic act got next to none.

Wallace not only spoke badly, he also looked tired and gloomy. His reception in Baltimore during the day must have been as far below his own expectations as it was below that of his attendants. They looked for an uproar of welcome in the Pennsylvania Avenue region, but what they got was not far from a frost.

Uniform Of Statecraft

He performed in the neat blue suit that is his usual uniform of statecraft, but it did not inspire him to anything even remotely approaching eloquence. Many an evangelist in the back-street tabernacles of Baltimore must have been praying ten times as loud last night as Wallace hollered.

In 44 years of listening to political rhetoricians I have never heard one make a punier or more ineffective speech.

Nothing more is to be said of his performance. It baffles journalistic science as certainly as it flabbergasted his audience. Obviously, at least some of those present looked for a chance to leap, howl and flap their wings. But no such chance came.

When he shut down at 10:22 o'clock, after running on for little more than half an hour, he turned from the mike and faded silently into the shadows behind him. The crowd seemed startled.

Few Linger On

After he was gone a few hundred lingered in the hall to greet Paul Robeson, the singer, who is traveling with the Wallace show and to badger him for autographs. While he was engaged in writing them at the edge of the platform, a white youth down in the hall began making a speech denouncing the Druid Hill Park mixed tennis episode and calling for contributions for the defense of those arrested.

He howled violently but the take was apparently meager. The whole of it, in fact, barely covered the bottom of a cigar-box. But he said that more than $100 had been raised outside.

He was followed by other orators, and for half an hour there was a mild hubbub, and the survivors of the main show had a chance to blow off their dammed-up steam. But then the lights in the hall began to blink, and it was all over. During the whole meeting the place had been in semi-darkness. The only strong lights were concentrated on the platform. Even the press-stand was almost inky dark.

Gets Off To Dismal Start

The exercises of the evening got off to a dismal start. At 8 o'clock, the time fixed for the jump-off, the 4,700 seats on the floor were only half occupied, and there was not a soul in the galleries. The crowd filed in slowly after that but there were plenty of empty chairs to the end.

Most of the vacancies were in the $2.40 and $1.20 seats, where three-fourths of the customers were white. In the cheaper seats to the rear dark faces were in a clear majority. The hall, in fact, was arranged as to color pretty much like a Jim Crow bus below the Potomac.

The crooners and gabbers who operated before Wallace's entrance were all feeble performers—all, that is, save his wiskinski, William S. Gailmor. Gailmor is a specialist at raising money, and he gave his usual good show. The others fell flat, including even Paul Robeson.

Robeson sang four lugubrious spirituals, and then did "Old Man River." After that he made a brief speech. He was received politely, but it would be an exaggeration to say that he knocked them out of their seats.

Wallace's Motives

Mencken Thinks Aim Is To Defeat Truman

SEPTEMBER 15—The Hon. Mr. Wallace's witless and sorry exhibition in Baltimore last Sunday night once more raised the question of his motives. It is hard to believe a man of any intelligence taking seriously the prophecies of triumph so loudly voiced by the highly dubious characters of his immediate entourage. And it is equally hard to imagine a man of decent raising and personal dignity getting satisfaction out of associating with the motley nonentities who seek to jump aboard his three-wheeled bandwagon.

So far as I have been able to make out not a single person of any importance whatsoever is running for office on his ticket, or giving him active support. From his candidate for the vice-presidency, the Hon. Glen Taylor, down to those who aspire to Congress or to local jobs inder his banner, they are all excessively inferior—ward heelers smarting under the neglect of the regular party bosses, college tutors who revolt against the rattan and nothingness, professional messiahs who urge this or that minority group on to glorious disaster, and such-like vacuums.

Taylor is at once the most conspicuous of these followers and the worst. A ham actor who took to politics when the radio ruined his art and mystery, he got into the Senate by one of those accidents that make politics so delightful, and has carried on there as a bad imitation of all the cow-state John the Baptists of the past.

He is cheap, vulgar and stupid. To look at him is to laugh; to hear him is to bust into tears. He is on the ticket for one reason only, and that is the reason that Wallace could not snare a more seemly running mate. The third- and fourth-raters all ducked, and there was nothing left save this preposterous fifth-rater.

Candidates for high office are notoriously willing to believe anything, and most of them, like the Liberals, are willing to believe anything twice. But though Wallace has this talent in a marked degree, and has even fallen, in the past, for oriental snakecharmers and rope-trick metaphysicians, it is impossible to think that he believes he can win in November. Indeed, if he cherished any such hallucination at the start, he must have been purged of it by the events of his campaign, which has been going everywhere as it went in Baltimore last Sunday.

Even the Jewish voters in the Bronx are plainly wobbling, and it will take a heavy effort by their two leaders, Congressman Marcantonio and Congressman Isacson, to hold them in line. As for his other bloc, the colored brethren, they are already in full flight. They gave him the cold shoulder on his tour of their settlements in Batimore, and judging by their response to his speech, most of those who attended his orgies at the Armory came out of curiosity, not in devotion.

One characteristic of the colored people is always overlooked by those who write about them, and that is their sense of humor. They are sometimes, just like the whites, caught in an overwhelming flood of demagogy, as when Roosevelt II fetched them, but as a usual thing they are suspicious of those who undertake to save them, and are not easily fooled. No other minority group among us is so intelligently critical of its leaders or voices its opinions, often low, with greater frankness.

Everyone who reads the Negro papers must have noted that they are dealing with Wallace warily and are not apt to succumb to him. They have heard all his baloney before, and know precisely what it is worth. If their editors really believed that he is even the half of what he pretends to be, they would be flocking after him, but they do not believe he is. Nor is he.

His alliance with the Communists, made manifest all over again at the Baltimore camp-meeting, has scared off all the colored eminentissimos save a few—for example, Paul Robeson—who are indistinguishable from Communists themselves, and the same capital folly has alarmed the rank and file. They know very well that if war with Russia comes, as seems most likely, everyone tarred with that stick will be in serious trouble, and they don't want to invite it. They would get the worst of any uproars set off by the Communists, and they know it.

But to return to Wallace's motives. Is he carrying on a laborious campaign in highly odoriferous company because he thinks he can snatch the ermine of Lincoln? I doubt it: he is not dumb enough. Does he, then, mourn for the down-trodden, and pant to comfort them? I doubt it again: he is a good deal less interested in working people than he is in labor racketeers.

Has he, to make an end, got his eye fixed on 1952, with hopes for a resurrection from the ashes and old bones of the next administration. Once more I doubt, for when third parties blow up they stay blown up, and no one knows it better than Henry Wallace.

Well, what is left? I can see nothing save a bitter hatred of Truman, and a vast itch for revenge on him. This, at worst, is logical and human. Poor Henry really has sound ground for hating Truman. It was Truman who did him out of the vice-presidency and Truman who kicked him out of the cabinet and public office. He can't win himself, but he can at least, he figures, drive a few nails into Truman's political coffin. This he is now trying to do. Unhappily, his hammer has a greased handle and may slip and mash his thumb.

Mencken In Gloomy Mood

View Of Candidates Leaves Him Uninspired

SEPTEMBER 22—The campaign, so far, has produced little save balderdash, and there is no visible sign that it will rise to better form hereafter. The Hon. Mr. Truman, in his harrying of the West, has confined himself to a cheap and obvious demagogy, none of it worth serious consideration. And the Hon. Mr. Dewey, as in 1944, seems bent only on proving that he is in favor of everything, however irrational, that his opponent is in favor of.

Dewey, I suppose, will win, but if he does it will not be because he has collared any considerable body of intelligent voters, but simply because Truman has alienated and disgusted them. He made his first campaign hanging on to the coat-tails of the New Deal, and in this one he has certainly not got very far behind its retreating hoofs. He has a vast capacity for swallowing perunas. If he can't get them down by normal deglutition he helps them on their way by a bold use of ramrods, mint-mashers and engine-oil.

An example is provided by his announcement that there is no difference in foreign policy between his own party and Truman's. What this actually means, of course, is that the American people, save for the Wallace Communists, are unanimously behind Truman.

It would be hard to imagine anything more absurd. The American people, in fact, are sharply divided on the subject, and probably enough of them to make a majority are convinced that Truman's handling of the Russians has been feeble and silly, and that they are thereby accumulating large advantages in the war that is plainly inevitable.

Wallace, if he had any sense, might be making effective practice against both Truman and Dewey, and so justify his existence as the leader of a third party. But Wallace, it is now manifest, has now lost what little sense he had formerly, if indeed he ever had any at all. The Communist half of his following has taken him for a dizzy ride, with a fatal smash only around the corner. His ideas, as he has been expounding them to shrinking audiences, are indistinguishable from those of the crooked labor racketeers, the Friends of the Stern Gang and the generality of the intellectually unemployed.

This leaves Norman Thomas and Thurmond, of South Carolina. Thomas, in so far as the newspapers are reporting him, seems to be talking sense, at least from the Socialist standpoint, but with Communists in the ring no one wants to listen to Socialists, who are to Communists as soda-pop is to 100-proof rye. As for Thurmond, an intelligent and honest man and probably the best of all the candidates, he is handicapped by the fact that all the worst morons in the South are for him.

His candidacy, to be sure, is not supported by such vermine exclusively. He also has the backing of some of the best men and women below the Potomac. But there are not enough of them to make any impression on the rest of the country. In such states as Mississippi, for example, persons notable for sense are so few that they hardly surpass the numbers of a coroner's jury or a corporal's guard.

Thurmond himself has been carrying on an enlightened campaign, and the chances seem to be good that his speech in Baltimore on October 1 will be better than anything that has been offered so far by his opponents. But he is handicapped, like Wallace, by his followers. Wallace has the Communists around his neck and Thurmond has the Ku Kluxers. Both are stupid, vicious and nefarious. Between the two, in truth, I think I'd rather take my chances with the Communists.

I suppose that many and many a voter, unable to stomach so shabby a mountebank as Truman or so limber a trimmer as Dewey, is wondering where to cast his vote November 2. In this emergency I wish I could come forward with astute and elegant advice, but I must admit at once that I haven't any to offer. It is my firm conviction, reached after long experience, profound pondering and incessant prayer, that no man who is worth a hoot will ever be president of the United States hereafter. We are doomed to suffer an endless procession of quacks—until, that is, the Republic itself blows up.

The odds against any really competent and forthright man getting the nomination are simply hopeless. In the Republican convention which chose Dewey there were probably at least a dozen potential candidates who were his superiors. I name only two—Vandenberg and

Taft. But he beat one of them easily, and the other was too wise to enter the race. So at the Democratic convention. There were present not a dozen but fully twenty men who were as clearly above Truman as Truman himself was above—but I duck the labor of finding someone Truman was above.

All these gentlemen, some of them open aspirants, had the dismal fate of so many ice-cream cones in a blast furnace. They frizzled and fried away in the glare of Truman's monumental trashiness. His immense unfitness for his job gave him a cinch on it. For the political knaves who make presidential candidates have a vast fear of any able and honest man and will have nothing to do with him if they can help it. Always, in late years, they have managed to help it, and I am full of confidence that they will likewise be able hereafter.

Of the candidates actually in the ring today I incline to think that Dewey is the best. He has some skill at administration, and the manipulators who work his wires are at least a cut above the Pendergast parolees who seem to run Truman. Moreover, he is full of hot ambition and may be trusted to exert himself once he is in the White House.

But not, I greatly fear, in the campaign. His boldness, such as it is, is not of that sort. He doesn't want to be put on the spot. He will keep a sharp eye on all the pressure groups.

If, heated up by his own rhetoric, he ever promises to chase any of them away from the public trough I shall be tremendously surprised—and infinitely tickled. Some time ago he was reported to have shied a brick at the political pedagogues—one of the worst gangs of tax-eaters now at large. Challenged, he ran for cover. But some day, if it be God's will, he may stand. At all events, let us hope so.

Mencken On Thurmond, Suh

Looks On Bull Run Ticket's Rally As Elegant But Futile

OCTOBER 2—It would be an exaggeration verging upon the super-colossal to call the Confederate pow-wow at the Lyric last night a riot of enthusiasm, but all the same Governor J. Strom Thurmond was pleasantly received, he made a dignified and intelligent speech, and he spoke to a highly respectable audience.

He has no more chance of carrying Maryland for his Bull Run ticket on November 2 than the late Billy Sunday had of carrying Hell, but he has some admirers here, and about 1,000 of them turned out at the Lyric. Most of them seemed to be elderly, and many of them were ladies. They almost but not quite filled the lower floor, they bulged into about half the box seats, and there were three in the gallery.

The exercises were of a very sedate and even somber character. They began with a crooner who warbled "The Old Folks at Home," "Carry Me Back to Old Virginia" and other such masterpieces of sub-Potomac hymnody, and then they went on to some equally depressing pieces by six union men in the orchestra pit.

File Silently On Stage

At eight forty-five precisely Governor Thurmond, his lovely wife, and about a dozen other followers filed solemnly upon the stage, and took their seats. Then up rose the Hon. Thomas F. Cadwalader to introduce the candidate. He came to him by way of Hitlerian Germany, New Zealand and other distant points, and got him to the mike at nine.

A Maryland flag and a Confederate flag, both small, were unveiled on the stage. Another Confederate flag flapped from a staff back in the audience. Two American flags hung at the two sides of the proscenium arch.

It was the first time in many years that any force of Confederates had invaded the Baltimore area. In fact, it hadn't happened since July, 1864, when Colonel Harry Gilmor and his cavalry swooped down on the Glenn L. Martin plant, and scared a great many Baltimoreans out of a year's growth.

Business Is Persuasion

But Governor Thurmond was not out to scare anyone. His business was persuasion, and he undertook it in a suave and gentle way. He is of slight build, his hair is beginning to yield to his 46 years, and his voice is quite without the surges and hullabaloos that mark the speech of most other southern statesmen. He spoke exactly like a high-toned lawyer performing in court—not before a jury, but before a court of appeals. He seldom rose above his middle register, and indulged himself in no gesture save an occasional stab with his right forefinger. Now and then there was a wave of polite applause, but no more. No one yelled.

His pronunciation was plainly southern, but it was nothing like Tidewater Virginian nor even like Charleston, South Carolinian. Rather, it was that of the South Carolina Up Country, where he was born and still has his being. The word *force,* which he used often in describing the diabolic schemes of Truman, Dewey, Wallace and the Communists, always became *foce*, and a good many other *r's* were elided. For the rest, it was very clear and altogether without rhetorical gasps and gurgles.

No Hint Of Demagogy

In brief, an elegant meeting—soft in tone, with no hint of demagogy, and proceeding from end to end with the decorum of a well-bred dinner party. The police, who turned up half expecting that the Wallace Communists might bust in to pay back a certain debt of eggs and tomatoes, soon concluded that there was to be nothing of the sort on the program, and so departed to resume their weary hunt of murderers.

Eschews Booze, Tobacco, Coffee

What was accomplished by the evening's pale orgies I am unable to make out. As I have said, the Thurmond leaders have no hope whatsoever of carrying Maryland, and may not even get a place on the ballot. There were no converts at the mourners' bench last night, and no one in the sedate and somewhat mousy crowd showed any sign of excitement, or even of being absorbed. The Hon. Galen Tait, until lately boss of the Maryland Republicans, was there, but everyone knows that he goes to the meetings of all parties, and that he has not been converted to anything for more than 50 years.

The newspaper reporters traveling with the candidate and his pallbearers brought the news that he is an ascetic of extraordinary virulence, even for a southern Baptist. He not only eschews booze and tobacco; he also keeps off coffee. I should add in fairness that he does not look it; one might reasonably imagine him dropping off at a lunch-wagon on a frosty morning for a cup of Arbuckles best or even sneaking a swig of corn behind the door.

He is also a Freemason, a Knight of Pythias, a Moose, a Woodman, a Lion and an ornament of the Junior Order of United American Mechanics, though how he qualifies as a mechanic I can't make out, for he has been a jobholder since 1929 and even before that he taught school, which is also a political office in South Carolina.

There is nothing of the low-down southern politician about him. He no more resembles the Talmadges, Longs, Bilbos and Pappy Daniels than he resembles a bookmaker. In brief, a gentleman. How far he hopes to get with his holy crusade for States' Rights I don't know, though last night he hinted darkly that it might throw the election into the House of Representatives. In national campaigns the candidates of third parties always cherish that hope. But it hasn't been realized in seven or eight hundred years.

Warren's Doctrine Found Impeccable—But No Zowie

OCTOBER 3—The Warren meeting at the Lyric last night is not likely to get much attention from historians. It was a Class C affair and when one has noted that it passed off without bloodshed nothing more need be said about it.

The vice-presidential candidate was introduced at 9 P.M. and launched into his prepared speech without further ado. All the while he was emitting it he held fast to the two sides of his pulpit.

It was a sensible speech, preaching sound and even impeccable doctrine, but there was no more zowie in it than there would have been in calling the roll.

Hearty And Handsome Fellow

The speaker appeared in a double-breasted gray suit, yellow shoes and a garnet-and-white necktie. He is a hearty and handsome fellow, with bold and good features, a smooth face and the stance and manner of a seasoned Rotarian.

His voice is clear, but there is very little resonance in it, and no one would call him an orator.

He was accompanied by his wife, a very good-looking woman, and by their daughter, a handsome gal in the full flush of young blond beauty. They listened to him politely, but inasmuch as they had heard him two or three thousand times before they were plainly not carried away by his observations.

The only candidate ever heard of who had the humanity to leave his wife at home when he went campaigning was Alf Landon, who parked Mrs. Landon in Colorado in 1936.

The wives of the rest of them have to listen to them day after day and night after night, just as the wife of the late Billy Sunday had to listen to him. But Mrs. Sunday could get some relief by bawling all the hymns that were lined out, whereas the candidatesses have to keep silent. The most they ever get out of it is a box or two of candy, a corsage of embalmed orchids, and the chance to meet a gang of lady politicians.

As a general thing, these lady politicians are dreadful spectacles, but it must be said for those in attendance last night that most of them were quite bearable, and not a few of them were downright sightly.

Impromptu Reception Held

They all met and admired Mrs. and Miss Warren when the formal ceremonies were over, and the candidate held an impromptu reception on the stage. It went off smoothly and without any disorder.

The crowd fell short of filling the Lyric. All the seats on the lower floor were occupied, and also all those in the boxes, but in the rear ranks of the gallery there was plenty of room.

The decorations consisted of the usual strident bunting, some pictures of Dewey and Warren, and a few very chaste and noninflammatory placards. If there were more than 100 colored folks in the house then I am going color blind. Perhaps a dozen of them were on the stage, along with all the notables of the various splinters of the Republican party.

Republican Decorum

As I have said, the governor's speech was aimed mainly at the higher cerebral centers, and hence did not provoke any frenzies of applause. There was some handclapping now and then, and once a woman toward the front of the house loosed a yell, but that was all.

As everyone knows, Republican crowds are always a great deal more polite and decorous than Democratic crowds. There are seldom any drunken men among them, and they do not strip off their coats. In particular, the Afro-Americans in them show a reserved spirit and elegant manners.

The meeting last night escaped the clammy, morgue-like air of the Thurmond soirée on Friday, but nevertheless it was pretty dull.

One Sick, One Lost On Shore

A band had been hired but it made little effort to entertain the incoming customers. Before it had used up any considerable amount of wind the Hon. Stanford Hoff called for order, and introduced the chairman, the Hon. Blanchard Randall, who delivered a brief discourse on the issues of the hour.

It was the plan, after that, that he put up the six state congressional candidates, but one was lost somewhere on the Eastern Shore, another sent word that he was sick, and of the other four only one had anything to say.

This exception was the Hon. James W. Miller, of the Fourth District, who was described on the program as a "business man and realtor."

Homely Wheezes Lack Time

He got off some homely wheezes that made the crowd laugh, and might have gone on prosperously for twenty minutes, or even half an hour, but time was running short, so he had to be chased away.

One of the other candidates, described as "a lawyer, farmer, soldier, county attorney and state senator," started off by saying that he felt like singing the French national hymn, and even quoted the first strophe of it in French, but no one encouraged him to bust into it.

Congressman J. Glenn Beall, who came at the end, had only three minutes, for by the time he got up Warren was already shuffling in the sand-box off-stage, but he kept within them very neatly.

Inquiry Into Final Causes

Sometimes I wonder, following political rhetoricians on their dismal rounds, what they hope to accomplish by such meetings.

If the idea is that people be inflamed to support a candidate by seeing him, then it would be more rational to parade him through the streets for four or five hours, accompanied by a powerful union band and with cuties in drum-majorette costumes passing out portraits of him.

A really bang-up meeting, of course, has some sense, for people like noise and excitement. And a bang-up speech by a competent rabble-rouser sometimes rings in their ears until election day.

Pianissimo Exhibition

But a quiet lecture by a man incapable of yelling, embodying ideas that everyone has been reading in the newspapers for weeks past—certainly it is hard to imagine such a pianissimo exhibition drawing any blood.

Also, I often wonder why politicians supposed to be adept animal trainers find it so hard to drive a really substantial herd into their pen.

There must be at least 20,000 men and women in Baltimore who hope and pray that the anticipated election of Dewey and Warren will provide them with comfortable places at the public trough, and relieve them for a long while from the curse of work.

Yet the best the so-called leaders of the GOP in Baltimore could do last night was to accumulate barely 2,500 of them.

War Scare In Campaign?

Mencken Suggests It May Be Used By Truman

OCTOBER 5—Having shot off all his demagogic bolts against gluttons of privilege, princes of pelf, slaves of greed and other such hobgoblins, and failed thereby to detonate the plain people, the Hon. Mr. Truman has only one more likely weapon in his arsenal. That, of course, is a war scare.*

The time is growing short, but he could still use it. Indeed, it would take no more than a few days to bring it into action, for nine Americans out of ten are already convinced that the Russians are incurable scoundrels and that war with them is necessary and inevitable. A few loud alarms, a few melodramatic gestures, and the ancient patriotic cry of "Stand behind the president!" would be heard again.

That the right hon. gentleman, with his back to the wall and sweat streaming from his every pore, is desperate enough to try this time-worn caper must be manifest. The only question is whether he has the courage. He himself proclaims almost every day that he is an intrepid fellow, but there is still some doubt that he is brave enough to climb so high upon the hog.

What stays him mainly, I suspect, is fear that the customers, tired of his divagations and vacillations, might decide that, if war it is to be, some better man is needed to carry it on. Very few people seem to have any genuine confidence in him. Even labor has plain doubts about him, and even those romantics who whoop for his civil-rights baloney do so with their fingers crossed. He is only too obviously a shallow fellow, and no one of any sense whatever believes that shallow fellows will be useful in the coming contest.

*Mencken's call for preventive war against the Soviets in this piece was considered so strong that the *Sun* editors appended a note, "In this article, as always, Mr. Mencken expresses his own views, not necessarily those of *The Sun*."

Truman has handled the whole Russian situation in a singularly feeble and inept way. On the one hand he and his goons have made faces at Stalin, and on the other hand they have let Stalin get away with murder.

Is he for the Communists or against them? It is really hard to make out. While billions of the taxpayers' shrinking dollars have been pouring out to make propaganda against them in Europe, he has not only done absolutely nothing against them at home, but has actually spent a large part of his energy blocking and reviling those who have had at them.

Certainly no one can know better than he does that Washington swarmed with Reds in the heyday of the New Deal. Some of the most important government agencies—for example, the National Labor Relations Board—they ran openly, and there was hardly a rathole in the town that they didn't get their noses into. More, they dragged along many thousands of jobholders who, though no believers in the Marxian balderdash themselves, saw which way the wind was blowing. It was fashionable to follow the party line. Moreover, it was wise.

Committees of Congress began to look into this scandal while it was at its height, and they have kept on ever since—trying to find out, not only who was working for the Kremlin in time of war, but who slopped over to days of so-called peace. What help has Truman ever given to this important business? None whatever. Instead, he has howled idiotically at those who have been trying to carry it on, and stretched and abused the powers of his office to prevent them from getting the evidence they seek.

It would be hard to conjure up a more scandalous spectacle. Why should a president of the United States go to so much trouble to protect miscreants who pulled against their country in time of war, and in many cases are still pulling against it today? La Eleanor and other such minor dupes have since recanted and promised to sin no more, but Truman keeps hard at it. The thing sounds impossible, but there are the plain facts.

Bearing them in mind, one begins to doubt that a war scare would work as well for Truman as it has worked in the past for some of his immortal predecessors. It might, in fact, backfire and mess him up. In other words, it might only augment the apparent resolution of the country to return him to the Pendergast Gang, and go on under some more seemly and plausible commander in chief. Nevertheless, it is still in his pocket, and when the wall behind him begins to grow really red hot he may be tempted to heave it.

Whether he does or he doesn't, it must be crystal-clear by now that we are in for a battle to the death with the Russian barbarians, soon or late, and probably very soon. There is simply no living with them in Europe, just as there is no living with their fans and agents at home. They are incurably dishonest and dishonorable. They mistake every show of common decency for weakness, and leap to take advantage of it in a cynical and brutal manner. Either they must be thrown back into their Asiatic wilds, or the life of all civilized peoples will become intolerable.

The only question remaining is whether we should go on enduring them for a while longer, or tackle them at once and have done with it. My own impression is that tackling them at once will be easiest in the long run. They have a large army in Germany and in their satellite states, but they are not, in fact, a people of any noticeable military prowess. The Finns fought them to a standstill, and if we had not supplied them in the last war and helped them by climbing on Hitler's back, he would have driven them to Vladivostok.

The longer the United States hems and haws the better they will be prepared and the harder it will be to knock them off. In any case it will be a tough war, but it will be a good deal tougher in two or three years than it is today. Behind it, as the Hon. Mr. Dewey has been saying of late, there will stand a really united country. We'll be able, at worst, to do enormously more damage than we'll have to suffer, and in the end, if we are lucky, there will be something resembling a civilized peace in Christendom.

Also, we should be able to get rid at last of the Communists who now make so much stink in the United States. They have been running on long enough.

Mencken Thanks Thomas

Rare Political Hullabaloo By Really Intelligent Man

OCTOBER 18—It is a pity that so few Baltimoreans heard the Hon. Norman Thomas when he hollered in this great medieval city Saturday night.

Hearing him, I hasten to add, would have done them little if any permanent good. They would have gone away, as they came, with more or less disabled minds, kidneys and morals. But while they were giving him ear they would have at least enjoyed a rare and exhilarating pleasure, to wit, that of listening to a political speech by a really intelligent and civilized man.

The hon. gentleman, as some may have heard, is the candidate of the Socialists (not Communists) for president of the United States. He has been their candidate, in fact, since 1928, and during that time he has roved and afflicted the country every four years, urging the great masses of the plain people to vote for him.

Not many have ever done so, and he allowed on Saturday that he didn't expect many to do so on November 2. Nevertheless, he keeps a stout heart, and on some dim tomorrow, he hopes and maybe even half believes, his remote heir and assign will actually horn into the White House.

His speech was delivered in a little L-shaped hall 45 steps up a steep stairway above a Chinese restaurant at 107 North Eutaw Street. The hall belongs to the International Ladies Garment Workers, who have come out officially for Truman, but are very hospitable to Socialists.

The decorations are austere. At the prompt side of the little stage is an American flag with a gilt fringe and at the O.P. side is a fire extinguisher rampant, pointed at the speaker's desk. Behind the desk are three chairs built of massive timbers stained black and greatly resembling the electric chair at Sing Sing. To one side is an upright piano.

The candidate came down from New York in the late afternoon and reached the Pennsylvania Station shortly before 9 P.M. He was met there by four official pallbearers, but one of them had to go to work on the night shift at Sparrows Point, so there were only three when he reached the hall.

He stalked in without ceremony, was politely applauded and listened for a few minutes to the terminal strophes of an harangue by an English comrade. Then, at 9:07, he launched into his speech.

It was extempore throughout, and swell stuff indeed. No Republican rhetorician in this campaign, to my knowledge, has ever delivered more effective cracks at the demagogy of the Hon. Mr. Truman, and no Democrat has done greater execution upon the limber trimming of the Hon. Mr. Dewey. Most of all, no one of either party has made a greater hash of the dismal baloney of the Hon. Mr. Wallace and his Communists.

It ran on for more than an hour, but it seemed far shorter than an ordinary political speech of twenty minutes.

It was full of adept and memorable phrases, some of them apparently almost new. It shined with wit and humor. The speaker poked gentle but devastating fun at all the clowns in the political circus, by no means forgetting himself. There was not a trace of rancor in his speech, and not a trace of Messianic bombast.

It was the sort of elegant spoofing that has not been heard on the stump in Baltimore since Charles J. Bonaparte was snatched to glory.

Unhappily, next to nobody heard it. The crowd in the hall barely filled the seats, and they certainly do not accommodate more than 150 head of customers. Even so, no converts were made, for all those present save a few abandoned newspaper reporters were already converted.

When Comrade Jerome I. Tucker, imitating Wallace's ferocious wiskinski, Comrade Gailmor, undertook to sweat the faithful for radio money, the most he could get, even with the help of a charming comradess, Miss Jean Martin by name, was less than $150 cash money. He stuffed it in his pants pocket with sincere rejoicing. It will be used, he said, in Cumberland, where radio time is cheap.

Thomas, who will be 64 years old two weeks after he is counted out in November, seems to be holding up very well. There is not much hair left on top of his head, and what remains behind is now snow-white. His life-long devotion to Talmudic and economic studies has bent him a little where his cervical and thoracic vertebrae meet, and there is a whisper of a paunch in front, but in general he looks brisk and chipper.

His voice is loud, clear and a trifle metallic. He never starts a sentence that doesn't stop, and he never accents the wrong syllable in a word or the wrong word in a sentence. His long, somewhat thin face is without foliage, and on Saturday looked bright and rosy.

Just how far he goes in accepting the Socialist whim-wham I do not know, though I have been reading him and listening to him for years.

There was not a single mention of Papa Marx in his remarks, nor of any of the other Socialist archangels. His position seems to be roughly analogous to that of the British Labor party, though I doubt that he swallows some of its more preposterous chicaneries. He regards most American liberals as jackasses, and is not backward about saying so.

If the cops heard of his meeting they apparently decided that it would produce no roughhouse, so they did not come to the hall. At the Wallace meeting in the 5th Regiment Armory a month or so ago they showed up in a dense swarm, commanded by half a dozen inspectors and with their hurry-wagons backed into nearly every alley.

No Communists, whether Wallace or dirt, were on hand to hear Thomas. The crowd was very decorous, and its star was a University of Maryland professor. He talked, too, but only very mildly. So did the English comrade. So did Comrade Tucker.

But the candidate really cut loose. I paid nothing to hear him; in fact, I was paid for doing so by The A.S. Abell Company, a soulless and highly solvent corporation, God save the mark.

But if it had cost me $2, or even $3, I'd have thought the money very well laid out. It is not often in this great Republic that one hears a political hullabaloo that is also a work of art.

Mencken On Barkley

A Competent Rabble-Rouser, But Plenty of Empty Seats

OCTOBER 23—The Democratic outpouring at the Lyric last night was a political hullabaloo of the middle sort—neither a smash nor a flop.

Great efforts had been made to turn out a record crowd, and the Hon. John O. Rutherford, clerk of the city court, had been sworn in as Simon Legree to round up and drive in every jobholder on the city payroll, but a good many of them escaped his whips, gamebeaters, trappers and cowhands, and there were plenty of empty seats in the hall.

The only lady politico heard from, Mrs. John L. Whitehurst, alleged from the platform that more than half of the patriots present were female, but this was a considerable exaggeration. The true number was probably between 20 and 25 per cent. Of Afro-Americans there were no more than two or three per cent and nearly all of them were in the very sparsely filled gallery.

A Solo Performance

Not much applause was heard during the exercises. There was a fan in one of the boxes who occasionally loosed a shrill exultation, but he gave a solo performance. At no time did the crowd let go with delirious plaudits. Waves of mild handclapping passed over the house at suitable places, but they never got beyond control. I have no doubt that a good deal more noise was heard at the dinner of the downtown committee, holden simultaneously at the Lord Baltimore Hotel.

The orator was the Hon. Alben W. Barkley, of Kentucky, candidate for vice-president on the Truman ticket. He had a speech in hand that had been prepared by his literati, and during the minor hollering that went on before he got to the mike he studied it diligently and with apparent interest, but he started off extempore and kept on mainly extempore to the end. At one time he grabbed up a whole fistful of his typescript and dropped it to the floor.

Stance Is Dignified

Barkley is a highly competent rabble-rouser, but he is also more than that, for his stance at the mike is dignified and he howls only at long intervals and then only briefly. His speech was mainly made up of lugubrious prophecies as to the fate of humanity if Truman is beaten on November 2, but inasmuch as a good 90 per cent of his hearers had apparently resigned themselves to that catastrophe, he caused no excitement.

A short, stocky fellow with a somewhat husky but nevertheless effective voice, he knows how to drive home his points. His hair is thinning, but he still has an adequate thatch of it; it is graying but not yet faded to white. He still reads without glasses, though he has to bring his manuscript close to his eyes. Once, when he seemed to be strangling on an extra-long sentence, Senator Millard E. Tydings leaped to his side and offered him a drink of water. "Thanks very much, Millard," he said, "but Iam from Kentucky."

Anti-Saloon League Cadet

He originated in the tobacco country below Paducah and got his start in statecraft as a cadet of the Anti-Saloon League. For a few years in his remote youth he practiced law, but since 1904 he has been continuously at the public trough—first as prosecuting attorney in his native wildwood, then as a county judge, then as a congressman, and finally as a senator. He entered the Senate on the same day that Tydings got in, and they were sworn upon the same Bible.

As soon as the New Deal dawned he became one of its most violent advocates, and was quickly marked for preferment. When old Joe Robinson died in 1937 Roosevelt II ordered that he be made majority leader of the Senate. This command was conveyed to the other Democratic senators, somewhat to their chagrin, in the famous "Dear Alben" letter, now cherished by historians as they cherish Lincoln's Gettysburg Address. He remained the majority leader until early last year, when the Republican landslide of 1946 reduced him to minority leader.

Pleasant Baritone Voice

In these offices he has shown a good deal of capacity. He is a smart debater and is seldom caught by the opposition with his suspenders not functioning. He had a large share in filing off some of the sharper teeth of the original Taft-Hartley Act, and fought long and hard against the various over-riding of Truman vetoes. He keeps his head when smoke is pouring out of the Senate, and is amiable and well-liked. In his hours of ease he lifts his voice in song. He has a pleasant baritone voice, and made musical history by leading the singing of "God Bless America" at the 1940 Democratic National Convention. He has never afflicted the country with any legislative hallucinations of his own, and no law to gouge the taxpayer bears his name.

His record on Prohibition well reveals his openness of mind. He voted for the submission of the Eighteenth Amendment in 1917, for the Volstead Act in 1919, and for the Jones Five-and-Ten Act in 1929, but when the dry millenium blew up in 1932 he got converted overnight and was presently voting for repeal. In brief, his principles are operated by sensitive antennae and coiled springs. He can believe anything that seems reasonable and judicious at the moment.

Term Runs Until 1951

When he got to Philadelphia last July Truman's choice for vice-president was Justice William O. Douglas, but when Douglas fled to the High Sierras in alarm, "dear Alben" was glad to take the nomination, at the same time giving thanks to God. He would probably make an excellent vice-president, if only because he is hep to every trick of senatorial chicane, but as it is he will have to be remembered along with Charlie Bryan, John W. Kern and Henry G. Davis. The event of November 2, however, won't upset him much, for his fourth term in the Senate runs until 1951, and by that time he will be pushing 75.

The rhetoricians who preceded him last night were the Hon. Robert B. Ennis, Governor Lane, Mayor D'Alessandro, the Hon. George Radcliffe and Mrs. Whitehurst. All of them sought to shake the prevailing gloom, but without much success. Ennis urged a row of standing jobholders at the back of the hall to take seats, but most of them remained standing.

The Hon. Galen Tait was hidden in the crowd, smiling his satanic smile. Though he is a Republican, he never misses a Democratic outpouring, especially when Democrats are feeling a little sick.

Two Truman Mistakes

Mencken Lists His Views On New Deal And Wallace

OCTOBER 26—The Hon. Mr. Truman's fundamental mistakes in the present campaign are not hard to see. For one thing he has greatly underestimated the extent of the reaction against the New Deal. And for another thing he has overestimated the Wallace movement.

It is the first error that will fetch him next Tuesday, but it is the second that best reveals his scattered state of mind. His insane plan to send Chief Justice Vinson to Moscow, to grovel before Stalin, can be explained only on the theory that he believed vast numbers of Americans had been convinced by Wallace that knuckling to the Kremlin assassins was the one way to avoid war.

This, alas, was a double imbecility. On the one hand Wallace had convinced vast numbers of Americans of precisely nothing. Instead, his shameless alliance with the Communists had persuaded the country that his whole body of ideas was dubious, the good along with the bad. And no person of elemental sanity believes that war can be put off, or made less onerous when it comes, by dealing with Stalin and company as if they were honest men.

Wallace, who is one of the most thumping asses ever heard of in American politics, ruined his party and the whole Progressive movement with it when he let the Communists muscle in on him. Before he called his so-called convention in Philadelphia, that movement seemed to be perking up, and he apparently stood a good chance of collaring most of the surviving followers of Roosevelt I and La Follette, and an even larger number of advocates and beneficiaries of the New Deal.

But when the Communists, emerging from their sewers, moved in on him in the clear light of day, he started down the chute, and before his campaign really began, he was going down at the rate of 100 knots. No worse gang of stinkers has ever been on public view since the days of the Know Nothings. The thought of letting them into the White House was revolting to every American of common decency—and, as the Hon. Mr. Warren was saying wisely in Baltimore a few weeks ago, most Progressives are decent, too. So, for all I know, are some of the New Dealers, though I have not had the good fortune to meet any of them.

In any event, both outfits took to the woods, and Wallace was left to his Moscow agents, many of them labor racketeers. He has been rocking down to disaster and oblivion ever since. The Communists have made a monumental fool of him. The more he argues that we should stand idly by and let them turn all Europe into a madhouse, the more he proves to reasonable men that he is a good man to vote against. He loses support every time he opens his mouth.

Truman's fear of this zany and his mephitic followers is but one more proof that Truman's capacity for sound judgment is very slight. He began as a ward heeler under the Pendergast gang, and he still shows all the childish qualities of a shoe-string politician. When, on the night of his nomination in Philadelphia, he leaped to the mike and delivered an angry and silly tirade against Congress, all he achieved was to convince everyone that he was scared. His extra session was a complete flop: the Republicans were altogether too smart for him. And they have been running rings around him ever since.

But he is surrounded by very bad advisers, and they have kept him howling his hollow demagogy. There is an excellent case against Dewey, but no one has heard any statement of it by Truman. On the contrary, he has confined himself to bawling against the Taft-Hartley Act, and to promising, if re-elected, to ruin every employer in the country.

I doubt that any considerable body of working men—I mean men who know and practice some useful craft, and want work, not doles—have been taken in by this fustian. The dream of bankrupting the boss does not fetch such men; they have seen what its realization has done to their fellows in Russia. It is cherished, not by actual workers, but by labor racketeers, and, what enchants those racketeers, only too plainly, is the itch to be promoted to commissars. Lolling in Florida and boozing away the workman's ever mounting dues, they envisage the day when the boss will go to the shooting cellars and the workman will be their slave.

The Taft-Hartley Act, despite its deficiencies—mainly due to

Truman—is aimed at these racketeers, not at the working man. Its primary purpose is to get a reasonable amount of sense and justice into the National Labor Relations Act, which, under Roosevelt, was a good deal more Russian than American. In large part, in fact, it was administered by Communists, and some of its operations were of an almost incredible unfairness.

I do not believe that any workman of ordinary self-respect ever approved this wholesale burlesque of justice, even when he happened to profit by it. In most cases, of course, he profited little or nothing. Its real beneficiaries were the labor racketeers. Protected by the Roosevelt Reds, they ran many of the unions despotically and dishonestly, and the great body of members were helpless against them. I am convinced that large numbers of good union men are tired of being kicked about by such criminals. In the long run they will be made better off under the new law than they were under the old one, and are well aware of it.

In any case, it must be manifest that Truman's effort to launch a class war upon the country has failed. People of any sense simply refuse to believe that the boss is now getting everything and the workman nothing. The boss, to be sure, is getting more than he got when New Deal taxes took it all, but he is not boozing it away in Florida: he is laying it out on new plants that will provide new and more secure jobs.

Truman has tried to convince the country that this is not so. He has failed ingloriously. His campaign has not been that of a statesman, nor even that of the wiser and decenter sort of politician; it has been that of a third-rate rabble-rouser. He has appealed, not to the common sense of the people as a whole but to the itch for advantage of vicious racketeers and prehensile and mainly highly dubious minorities. If he gets a good licking on Tuesday he will surely deserve it.

Truman's Election

Mencken Says Country Jolly Well Deserves It

NOVEMBER 7—The super- or ultra-explosion that staved in the firmament of heaven last Tuesday not only blew up all the Gallups of this great free Republic; it also shook the bones of all its other smarties. Indeed, I confess as much myself. Sitting among my colleagues of the *Sunpapers* as the returns began to come in, I felt and shared the tremors and tickles that ran up and down their vertebrae.

How could so many wizards be so thumpingly wrong? How could the enlightenment play so scurvy a trick upon its agents? Certainly there must have been very few Americans in the IQ brackets above 35 who actually expected Truman to win. I met a great many politicos during the campaign, some of whom whooped for the right hon. gentleman and some of whom whooped against him, and yet I can't recall a single one who showed any sign of believing that he could beat the rap.

Even his running-mate, the Hon. Alben W. Barkley, who hollered in Baltimore on October 22, was plainly full of doubts. A professional jobholder and rabble-rouser for 43 years, he did his stuff as in duty bound, but if there were any high hopes welling within him he certainly kept them concealed from the customers. His general air was that of a country pastor preaching the funeral services of a parishioner plainly bound for hell, and all the other jobholders present looked and acted a good deal more like pallbearers than wedding guests.

But, meanwhile, the Missouri Wonder was roving and ravaging the land, pouring out hope and promise in a wholesale manner. To the farmers he promised a continuance of the outrageous prices that are reducing the rest of us to eating only once a day. To the city proletariat he promised ever higher and higher wages, with the boss a beggar at his own gate. To the jobholders he promised more and more jobs, and juicier ones. To the colored brethren he promised the realization of their fondest hopes and hallucinations. And so on to the glorious end of the chapter.

What had Dewey to offer against all this pie in the sky? Virtually nothing. His plan in the campaign, as in that of 1944, was to chase what appeared to be the other fellow's ambulance. He seemed eager to convince everyone that he was for everything that Truman was in favor of, but with much less heat. Never once in his canvass, so far as I can recall, did he tackle Truman's buncombe and blather in a frank and forthright manner. His speeches were beautiful songs, but all of them were sung *pianissimo.*

His literati have been blamed for this tender gurgling, but it seems to me that the fault was all his own. The late Al Smith, in the campaign of 1928, was afflicted by literati even more literary, but he got rid of them by tearing up their speeches and striking out on his own. To be sure, he didn't win, but that was surely not because he did not make a good fight; it was simply because the Bible searchers everywhere had become convinced that if he got to the White House the Pope would move into the cellar.

Dewey had no such handicap and yet he came to grief in the grand manner. His defeat ran against all the probabilities and was complete, colossal and ignominious. Its springs, I believe, are to be sought in defects of his own personality. He is by nature cute but cautious. He is a good trial lawyer, but an incompetent rabble-rouser. He addresses great multitudes as if they were gangs of drowsing judges, all of them austere in their hangmen's gowns, but consumed inwardly by an expectant thirst.

Truman made no such mistake. He assumed as a matter of course that the American people were just folks like himself. He thus wasted no high-falutin rhetoric upon them, but appealed directly to their self-interest. Every one of them, he figured, was itching for something, and he made his campaign by the sempiternal device of engaging to give it to them. A politico trained in a harsh but realistic school, he naturally directed his most gaudy promises to the groups that seemed to be most numerous, and the event proved that he was a smart mathematician.

Neither candidate made a speech on the stump that will survive in the schoolbooks, but those of Truman at least had some human warmth in them. Like Al Smith, he frequently disregarded the efforts of his literati, and proceeded on his own, and it was precisely at such times that he was most effective. While Dewey was intoning essays sounding like the worst bombast of university professors, Truman was down on the ground, clowning with the circumambient morons. He made votes every time he gave a show, but Dewey lost them.

One of the most significant phenomena of the campaign was the collapse of Henry Wallace's effort to convert the plain people to the Russian whim-wham. They simply refused to be fooled, and if the battle had gone on for another month his support would have been reduced to the Communists. At the start Truman was plainly afraid of him, but only at the start. It soon appeared clearly that all the actual Progressives behind Wallace were made uneasy by the Communists' collaring of him, and in the end most of them were fetched by Truman.

He was out to get all the softheads, and he got them triumphantly. Unhampered by anything resembling a coherent body of ideas, he was ready to believe up to the extreme limits of human credulity. If he did not come out for spiritualism, chiropractic, psychotherapy and extra sensory perception it was only because no one demanded that he do so. If there had been any formidable body of cannibals in the country he would have promised to provide them with free missionaries fattened at the taxpayers' expense.

So we now have him for four years more—four years that will see the country confronted by the most difficult and dangerous problems presented to it since 1861. We can only hope that he will improve as he goes on. Unhappily, experience teaches that no man improves much after 60, and that after 65 most of them deteriorate in a really alarming manner. I could give an autobiographical example, but refrain on the advice of counsel. Thus we seem to be in for it. I can only say in conclusion that the country jolly well deserves it.

Composed in Palatino by the New Republic Book Company, Inc.
Printed and bound by The Maple Press Company, York, Pennsylvania.
Designed by Gerard Valerio.